DALLAS

STICK TO YOUR GUNS,
MY FRIEND!

David Sauer

Dear James,

Best of luck
to your future.

[signature]

# THE UNITED UTOPIAN STATES OF AMERICA

## LIFE IN A LIBERAL'S PERFECT WORLD

### TWENTY-ONE THINGS LIBERAL ELITES ARE DOING TO UNDERMINE THE FABRIC OF AMERICA

### by
## Dave Sampson

Bloomington, IN  Milton Keynes, UK

authorHOUSE

*AuthorHouse™*
*1663 Liberty Drive, Suite 200*
*Bloomington, IN 47403*
*www.authorhouse.com*
*Phone: 1-800-839-8640*

*AuthorHouse™ UK Ltd.*
*500 Avebury Boulevard*
*Central Milton Keynes, MK9 2BE*
*www.authorhouse.co.uk*
*Phone: 08001974150*

*First published by AuthorHouse 7/7/2006*

*ISBN: 1-4259-4561-9 (sc)*

*Printed in the United States of America
Bloomington, Indiana*

*This book is printed on acid-free paper.*

*Author photograph taken by Jill Law.*

# Contents

Section 1: The United Utopian
States of America?

## Section 2: Where Do We Go from Here?

## Conclusion

# INTRODUCTION

On an increasingly frequent basis I hear news stories that make me shake my head and question the motives behind some of the asinine decisions regarding this country's laws and policies. These decisions are usually made by liberal judges and elitist policy makers to break down the fabric of America by weakening the power of the common man's individual rights. Liberals increasingly pander to the rights of the special interest groups and their fellow elites in our society. Elite bureaucrats pursue increasing amounts of power while doing all they can to limit our personal rights and freedoms. Over the past couple of decades we've seen what shape our nation has taken as a direct result of the Liberal's demented agenda. Without interference from the Right, our country will continue to weaken and crack under the destructive guidance of the Left.

This book depicts what a nation formed by the ongoing progression of elitist thought might look like. It also points out many of the frightening things that are already taking place in the United States today. These are the necessary steps the Liberals must take to form the utopian world in which the Left wants us all to live in, in the not-so-distant future. The catch? They must first destroy the society in which we now live.

Though the various actions and decisions made thus far, by liberal elites, have been no less than ridiculous, they have been put into place and are now policy, law, or at the very least, the new "Politically correct" way of looking at things. We have been slowly conditioned to unwittingly abide by the social system the Left has instituted in our country. Many citizens have been led like sheep, to accept ideas and lifestyles that are in direct opposition to the health and vitality of our nation. There are plenty of things that have been done by Liberals to weaken the fabric of America. Still, they have just begun to shake the foundation of the nation. It's not too late to stop them from destroying America, but we must act now. We currently teeter on the edge of societal decay. Every day we don't act against the Left's agenda is another day our children and our society slide nearer to the evils that await us on the other side of the proverbial edge.

In order to reshape the way an entire country thinks and lives, the Elites must first destroy the country in which we now live. By systematically breaking down time honored beliefs and traditions, liberal elites decide what us "Common folks" should think and celebrate. While granting special rights to small groups of minorities in our population, the elite Left continues to mitigate the importance and need for individual rights among the rest of us. Once decimated, they can tell us all that the archaic belief in Democracy has run it's course and that now; a more advanced and intelligent system of government rule can be instituted.

Sound kind of paranoid? Maybe a bit extreme? If you take notice of the headlines in today's newspapers and the reports on national news broadcasts, one can begin to see how the fabric of our society is being tested and stressed each and every day.

The fabric of America! Every time you hear of an activist judge that (because of the offense taken by one or two people) rules to ban a celebration recognized by millions of Americans, think of that fabric. When legislators vote to limit your rights while expanding their individual power, think of that fabric. When restrictions are placed on your ability to express free thought and voice you personal beliefs, think of that fabric. When your freedom of religion is replaced by freedom from religion, think of that fabric.

You're about to read the top twenty-one things that Elites are attempting to do to change the social and economical well being of America. Unfortunately, they are starting to see success with parts of their plan and this only encourages them to further push the boundaries of our tolerance. Of course there are many things that Liberals are doing to destroy the fabric of our country, but if we can slow the progress of the twenty-one things listed here, we're off to a good start in reclaiming our country.

Liberal elites have gathered to share their intellectually "superior" ideas with each other in the nation's capital. While they plot in D.C. to do harm to the nation they're supposed to represent, villages across the country are looking for their idiots!

It is going on daily around the country. Elites, who have little tolerance for "Simple-minded blue-collar folks," are working diligently to stifle and silence us. Once they've accomplished that goal they can continue, unimpeded, in their pursuit of the perfect world, their new utopia that is projected in the pages to follow.

# The United Utopian
# States of America?

I guess opinions would vary as to what the "Perfect world" would be. To some it might be a society free of crime, drugs, violence and stress. Others may see the perfect world as a very religious and highly spiritual society. A perfect world to terrorists might include daily car bombings, chaos, murder and fear. To an outdoorsman perhaps a log cabin in the forest and for an environmentalist an all-metal and plastic bio-dome in the city. To a Conservative it would be a society of free enterprise and common sense and to a Liberal, social programs and pre-ordained thought.

The point is there is no "One perfect world" for all. It is far too broad a stroke to paint a prefect world for the Muslim and the Christian, for Asian and Hispanic, for scholars and laborers or for Liberals and Conservatives. There are a hundred things that would differ if you asked a dozen people what their idea of a perfect world is. Therefore, it is impossible for liberal leaders to follow through with their promises of fixing what they may see as society's problems in order to make our world a perfect place. Utopia is unreachable and will be forever elusive due to the complicated and varied visions of a "Perfect world."

As seen through my eyes, a perfect world would be one of unlimited hunting and fishing opportunities. Gun laws would punish criminals that use firearms in crimes while granting law-abiding citizens every right insured to us by our founding fathers.

I'd like to see the timber industry put back to work by lifting all of the senseless logging and land-use restrictions implemented by former presidents, activist judges and environmental extremists. I'd like to abolish social programs that pander to able-bodied individuals and keep them more willing to accept a hand-out than a job. I'd reduce fuel prices and our dependence on foreign oil by establishing drilling fields that would allow us to tap into our own natural resources. Taxes would be greatly reduced for all income brackets because government waste and bloated social programs would be reduced.

You may think my perfect world sounds like a place you'd like to live. Someone else might like to kill me for my earth-raping, pro-gun, anti-PETA utopia. They in turn might wish for a world that I wouldn't much like to live. A place where no gas burning engines are used, everyone is a vegetarian, and nobody has to work to make a living.

Until the impossible happens and all humans are carbon copies of each other without free will and individual thought, utopia will evade mankind. No matter what type of utopia is promised to you by liberal politicians, they will never be able to deliver because of differences in philosophy and the perception of perfection. Although common sense tells us a perfect world is impossible, lets take a look at what the Liberals impossible perfect world might look like.

# Utopia Goal Number 1
## Social(ist) Healthcare?

Let's kick this shindig off by talking a little bit about the Liberal's favorite pet project. This endeavor has been one of obsession and bitter battles fought by Liberals to establish the granddaddy of all social programs. We're talking about "Universal health care," A.K.A. "Social medicine." To Liberals, it is the ultimate in providing care and compassion to the citizens (legal and illegal) of this fine nation. To Conservatives, it appears to be exactly what it is, another step towards creating a national dependence on the government.

Of the options offered to improve our current medical care situation; it makes sense to consider improving the medical system that we currently have in place that has served us for many years. Why reinvent the wheel? For example, our liberal friends want to reinvent the entire way medicine is practiced and covered by insurance companies by promoting Universal Healthcare. Instead, we need to improve the current health care system by working with HMO's, insurance companies, pharmaceutical companies and doctors to polish what is already in place. No, it won't be the social medicine that Liberals want, but American's don't want, nor could we afford the new system dreamed up by liberal believers in utopian healthcare. Admittedly, the medical system in this country could be improved. Work needs to be done in numerous areas of the medical care system to facilitate a more user-friendly system. This is a given, but Liberals see the system as broken beyond repair.

Claims that the system fails seniors, low-income folks and patients dependent on prescriptions are exaggerated, overblown and taken out of context. Liberals and the media do this to frighten the most vulnerable individuals in our society. By creating a panic and then promising a "fail-safe" solution, they hope to coerce support for their pet project. Better yet, they claim their proposed medical system will be free. Say the word free to *anybody* and you'll see ears prick up and eyes pop open. Many may be so enthralled by the mention of free health care they forget the old adage that "Nothing in life is free."

Personally I don't see the current medical system as all that bad. Improvements are always welcome, but I'm obviously too stupid to know what is good for me. It doesn't seem unreasonable to me that when I need to see a doctor I schedule a doctor appointment. A day or two later I visit *my* doctor, receive a bill from my insurance company for a fraction of the actual cost and go on living my life. This does not seem broken or even inconvenient. It costs me a bit more per month than I'd like to pay, but that's the way it is.

The Universal Heath Care Plan proposed by Liberal leaders such as New York Senator Hillary Clinton and Massachusetts Senator John Kerry among many others, promises to solve every known problem, as well as any unforeseen future problems that may arise in the American medical care arena. Not only are they promising free healthcare and psychic solutions to problems yet unknown, they are telling us it will have none of the drawbacks that Canada's socialized medicine has. The cost to implement such a system would figure in the billions of dollars. Yet liberals tell us that Universal Health Care would be free care for all.

Doctors currently making deserving wages based on fields of practice, experience and expertise would presumably be paid the same as interns and freshman practitioners. A heart surgeon shouldn't expect to make any more money than a podiatrist and a rural family practitioner could do as well as any medical university's chief of staff. I'd also assume there would be little chance for financial advancement under the new system. Why would a medical student go through years of training and incur countless thousands of dollars in student loan debt to pursue a career in a field where personal profit and advancement were so restricted?

How would drug companies fund research of new and improved prescription drugs if they were forced to surrender their long researched drugs to the government for a ridiculously low pre-set amount? How would drug manufactures regain money spent on R&D if the there is no charge for their product? How would investors in drug companies make any profit? How would the loss of profit in the medical field affect the nation's economy? How would Liberals afford the billions needed to start this wonderful new granddaddy of all Social programs?

Lets assume universal healthcare was actually established in the Liberals new utopia. With the new system in place hospitals could run 24-7/365 with no overhead costs. Everything from the electricity bills to the cost of doing laundry, from equipment to toiletries and from cafeteria food to waiting room magazines would be paid for with Federal Government dollars. The savings realized by thousands of hospitals and medical practices across the nation would be staggering. Of course the doctors would see no more of these savings in their paycheck. The nurses would not receive higher pay. Nor would the accountants, secretaries, janitors, or food service workers. As a matter of fact, smaller wages with smaller pay difference gaps would be designated. There would be a flat pay scale for each profession within the hospital. Let's use the following arbitrary figures for an example. Doctors might make a salary of, say, $45,000 per year, Nurses $32,000, Secretaries $25,000, Janitors $ 20,000, etc. The end result would be savings passed directly to the client receiving medical assistance. With drastically reduced salaries being paid to those in the medical professions, could Liberals possibly live up to their promise of free medical care for all?

The problem comes when Liberals run out of money as a result of not charging for services rendered and by spending huge amounts of money to run government funded medical facilities. I have yet to hear a proposal for ongoing funding of this system. My guess is that anyone making a decent wage as a result of education and hard work, would be taxed excessively.

If Donald Trump and Bill Gates could receive the same care as an 80-year-old widow, for the same price of nothing, something is wrong. Of course Mr. Trump and Mr. Gates would pay even more astronomical taxes than they already do to accommodate the "free" program. They may be forced to pay enough in taxes to make them think about folding up shop and moving on. All in the name of *free* medicine.

A comparison: It seems a lot to me like a friend telling me he'd like to take me to the best fishing hole in the state to catch the biggest fish in the lake and inviting me to join him on a certain date. It would not be until I arrived at the meeting spot that I'd then learn he didn't know where the lake was, what type of fish we'd be going after, that he didn't have a boat, or even a truck to haul the boat if he'd had one. A promise without a strategic plan is simply empty talk. Like my fishing buddy, Liberals talk about all the wonderful programs they'd institute if given the chance. Yet never have I heard a solid plan to fund or create a viable structure for these ideas. It's just talk. It's stated with conviction and fervor, but with little, if any plan to institute action.

Regardless of the promises made by Liberals (wearing those rose-colored glasses), the whole concept of universal health care goes against the grain of American society. In this land of freedom and self-sufficiency it would be nearly impossible to force this type of Socialist medicine on the citizens of America. That's not to say there isn't a small portion of the American population that would like nothing more than to have the government take care of any and all of their healthcare needs. Some people feel absolutely fine relying on others for their perceived wellbeing. Even these individuals, who currently see nothing wrong with big government running the healthcare system that they depend on, would surely be dissuaded with just a little education on the matter. The whole concept is nothing more than a blatant attempt by Liberals to put the government in control of yet another aspect of your life.

Liberals require no accountability or responsibility from those who benefit from even the least expensive healthcare systems. Currently, Oregon is seeing a large drop in the number of individuals who are on the Oregon Health Plan. This is medical insurance for low-income Oregonians. When the rules recently changed regarding payment policies for the plan, there was outrage among clients and advocates alike.

Though individuals are now required to pay a little money each month for coverage, we've seen participation in the program drop drastically. The shocking price raise? The cost went from zero, to an average of six dollars per month, for coverage. Advocates for the poor claim that even six dollars is too much to "force" low-income folks to spend on their own health care costs. The fact is, many clients refuse to sacrifice a trip to the movies or two packs of cigarettes or a six-pack of beer each month to cover the ridiculously low co-pay for their health care coverage. Am I alone when I say I have a difficult time justifying the costs to tax payers in continuing to support such an individual? This shows just how little personal responsibility the Liberals hold these individuals accountable for. Although definitely not limited to healthcare, the removal of personal accountability from those benefiting from low-income programs is amazing. Without even knowing it, these individuals are trading their independence for ongoing reliance on the government. It would scare the hell out of me to trust my health and the health of my family to these pompous Elites.

Can you imagine having to put in a request to visit a doctor for an ache or pain that you have. The request may take a week or more to be approved and then you'd receive an appointment date for days, weeks, or even months later. You'd be told which doctor would treat you and where they were located. The doctor-patient relationship would be about as personal as a form letter and you'd be stuck with that doctor regardless of your opinion of him/her. Things would be even worse with an individual who had a chronic illness or who required ongoing medical attention. There would be little time for personal attention when the system runs the public through the system like cattle. For a reference, look at our neighbors in Canada.

These issues really don't concern the Elites who want to "Take care" of you. As stated before, their goal is to create a social program to top all others. Your reliance on them is a key step to creating the new utopia they've so long dreamed of.

With the government now anxious to control your options for health care, and already in charge of food stamp allocations, rental assistance and cash allotments to low-income folks, we are headed down a road of total reliance. Being forced to relinquish self-sufficiency and pride of independence comes at great cost to society. As long as

Elites aspire to rule over the citizens of this country, the Left will justify it.

So it is with the Universal Health Care Plan that Americans don't know they need, don't want and couldn't afford, even if it were possible. Again, the health of the nation is not what drives the Liberals to implement this plan. Instead, it is the need and obsession of the Left to force reliance on the government. Liberals are planning the perfect medical system for the new utopia. For whom I don't know, but I'm sure to a few people out there this system would be perfect.

# Utopia Goal Number 2
# Kiss God Goodbye?

Another huge change in the Liberals new utopia would be the banning of the belief in God (or at least any mention, private or public, of His name) among all citizens. Secularists would be an ever-increasing sector of the new population. Not that a person who looks now can't see this already taking place. It happens in our schools, our city halls and most importantly in our courts. It threatens the very beliefs and ideals that formed and built this nation. Of course all the "Extreme" secularist ideas we are confronting now would be the common ideas shared among citizens in the new utopia. The idea of atheism, or at least agnostic beliefs, could be forced on our kids in public schools. Since neither is Christianity, there would be no church and state conflict to mention. Sound a little like the "indoctrination" the Left accuses Christians of?

## Schools

Already we're being forced by activist judges to trade the sacred age-old holidays like Christmas for the new fangled "Winter Holiday." Children's school Christmas pageants may no longer contain songs that mention God, Christ, Jesus, or the Virgin Mary. Manger scenes that depict the birth of Jesus are not only banned but highly denounced as ultra-offensive, practically a clove of garlic to a vampire. Not only have they taken the center of the holiday's celebration away due to "Church and state" conflicts, they've also taken away the festive symbols that represent Christmas to kids across our country. A small group of citizens and a handful of activist judges have had great success. In addition to taking Christ out of Christmas, they were also so offended by Santa Claus, Reindeer, Elves and Snowmen, that they were able to get these repulsive figures out of school pageants as well. I wonder how long it will be before some activist judge decides that snowflakes are a reminder of Christmas and bans snowstorms from forming in the month of December.

With generous consideration for the other 99 percent of Americans who want to celebrate Christmas, judges have left a few frills for these pageants. As far as I know, decorative lights may still be displayed on the stage. Tinsel and garland may be used for decoration as long as they are not colored red, green, gold, or silver. Christmas songs may be sung as long as they contain no mention of Christmas. Gifts may be exchanged as long as every gift is the same and financial aid was made available to any student who couldn't afford the nominal gift price.

In Washington D.C., the annual lighting of the nations Christmas tree kicks off a season of good-will, love and enjoyment of the holiday season. The national Christmas tree is a symbol of our belief in and celebration of Christ, as a nation. This year the symbol of faith, strength and spirit formerly known as the national Christmas tree, will change it's name. Offense taken by a few minorities, and lawsuits ruled on by activist judges, have forced our country to rename the most traditional of Christmas symbols.

Our new "Holiday Tree" looks the same as the Christmas tree did. It's just a tall and just as full as the Christmas tree. It holds the same lights and decorations that the Christmas tree did. It's located at the same place the Christmas tree was. But due to ridiculous claims by a few minorities who live in a country that allows them to make claims without being killed by government officials, you and I no longer have a Christmas tree. Who gave Muslims and Indians and Atheists the right to take away our traditional holidays? Like any special interest group, give them an inch and they'll take a mile!

We're told that it's the considerate thinking of a progressive and evolving society that makes offending others so offensive. If a Muslim is offended at the mention of God and an Atheist is offended at a manger scene, or if a Buddhist cringes at the talk of Santa Claus, then it is our duty as compassionate neighbors to quit believing in these things. If we don't want to, then we have judges who make laws that leave us little choice. Merry Christmas.

In the state of Washington, at least one school has banned the celebration of Halloween. That's right... a holiday celebrated by sweet-toothed kids for scores of years is now under attack in the liberal state of Washington. The school board found that the celebration of Halloween might be offensive to the religion practiced by witches. Honest to...let's not say God here... the little ghouls were thought to be a threat the Wicken religion practiced by witches. Yet there were no witches that said they were offended by the celebration of Halloween. They even thought the school board's decision was ridiculous. One elitist school board member who didn't like the Halloween holiday decided to use the *possibility* of offending a certain minority group and just like that Halloween is canceled for the entire school.

Easter will be our next battle to keep a Christian holiday intact. We, of course, will lose. It might not be this year but possibly the next. Activist judges will hear from some liberal parent in Los Angeles or New York about how the Easter Bunny scared their child or the mention of resurrection threatened their religious beliefs, and the holiday will be no more. If we're lucky we will be allowed to celebrate a "Spring Holiday." It won't matter that an overwhelming majority of Americans see this as one of the most important holidays in the Christian religion. Never would it be suggested in this great "Land of the free," to ban the celebration of Ramadan or Hanukkah. That would be so out of line the Liberals would nearly trample each other on the way to disbar the judge who ruled that these culturally sensitive holidays were now banned. Just as "Equal rights" pertain only to minorities, "Religious rights" seem to pertain only to non-Christian religions. Dare I suggest that Liberals here are at risk of sounding hypocritical?

Can you imagine the outrage and offense taken by minorities (who practice non-Christian religion) if it were decided they could no longer celebrate their religious holidays? How insensitive would that be? To force these rules on the majority is justified. To do it to a minority group is damnable at best. Only minorities can act offended and garnish attention from the Left. The rest of us should practice sensitivity to other cultures and their religions while walking softly around our own traditions. The last thing we want to do is offend *them*.

## Courts, Judges, and Society

Another attack on Christianity hits at the core of our morality. Morality will not be a big issue in the new utopia. The Ten Commandments that have sat in courthouses throughout the land for decades and centuries are now falling like dominoes to the rulings of liberal activist judges. Oh sure, they claim it's a church and state issue but what it boils down to is they don't like the message that the Ten Commandments project. They don't want to be told who to worship. They don't want to be reminded that they shouldn't be sleeping with their neighbor's wife. Stealing should be acceptable if it can be justified.

This is just the beginning of the moral decay to come in the new utopia. Our young generations are already so close to going over the proverbial edge that it may take a miracle to pull them back to reality. It's a "Do it if it feels good" generation brought into the world by the "Screw you" generation fathered by the "Question authority" folks from the 1960's. Right and wrong are fuzzy to youth today because right and wrong were never taught as solid ideas by their parents. It goes to figure that if they don't know right from wrong, they can do whatever they want, whenever they want to and their actions will have no consequence. With God out of the picture to keep people's moral judgments in check, society will become a modern day Sodom and Gomorra type free-for-all.

Courts currently judge a killer's insanity plea based on whether or not the defendant knew "right from wrong at the time of the crime." If entire generations can't differentiate between right and wrong then I assume that legally, they are all insane. If my thinking seems flawed here, look at the headlines in today's newspapers. Are you getting tired of seeing headlines like these?

"Student arrested for plotting teachers murder."
"Serial killer caught after 13th body discovered."
"Parents killed by angry child."
"Two teens shoot dog with arrow."
"Clerk killed, young thief gets $47.00."
"Teen drinking party claims the lives of three."
"Seven killed by student on junior high-school campus."
"High school drug ring ruined lives."
"Campus rape on the rise at state universities."
"Body of newborn found in nightclub dumpster."

If these headlines don't seem like the results of acts committed by insane people then I don't know what does. The problem is these headlines are so commonplace in today's society that they've lost their shock value. Fifteen years ago these headlines would have brought attention, action and questions about the moral state of our society. Today they are just stories that happened in some other state to some other people.

God, or American's silly belief in God, is a threat to the progression of the Elite's utopia. The realization that there is something larger and more powerful than oneself irritates the Left. Elites feel that in some way, they themselves are deities and that leaves little room for the belief in a higher power. An almost universal belief among America's citizens in God gives strength and unity to the masses. This is a huge speed bump on the highway to developing the new utopia. A society that believes in God will be a society that has standards and moral accountability. It will also be a society that has respect and common sense. These are not the conditions required to accomplish the liberal agenda of chaos, rebellion, and "Progressive" thought. Therefore, it is necessary for Liberals to eliminate or at least greatly reduce America's collective belief in God. The asinine examples listed in the previous pages of this chapter are just the beginning of the efforts to remove God from a highly religious society. Examples of these efforts in the near future will be even more shocking and appalling than what we've witnessed thus far. What the Elites fail to realize is that regardless of their protests, their lawsuits, their blasphemy and their refusal to tolerate Christians, God will never be banned from a Christian's heart. Therefore, Christians will always possess the qualities that the Elites are trying so hard to eliminate from our society.

Religion is the ultimate example of the Liberal's hypocrisy. We are now conditioned from the time we start school, to be tolerant and acceptant of other people's beliefs and customs. Elites have mandated that you and I hold no ill will towards those with ideas or beliefs that differ from our own. We are told that no matter what a person or group of people choose to do or believe, it is their right as an

American to do so. All sexual orientation is to be not only accepted, but also approved of. Laziness is not the fault of an individual and should not be frowned upon. Abortion is a woman's choice and therefore the murder of a child is acceptable. Yet when our ideas, opinions or beliefs differ from anyone else's, we're told that we're intolerant and that we don't have the right to voice *our* thoughts. Elites are conditioning us and attempting to retrain our morality in an effort to force us to be acceptant and tolerant. The hypocrisy comes when Liberals preach to us the acceptance of other religions and how important it is to groups of immigrants to retain and practice their religions and cultural customs. That's great! But Christians practice the religion and customs that formed the very nation that protects the religious rights of immigrants. Now *we* are being discriminated against. By whom, you may ask. It's being done by the very Elites who condition us to be ultra-tolerant of everybody else's beliefs . To accept deviant, or at the very least, poor behavior while condemning the values of Christianity is what Liberals are persuading our youth to do. It's wrong and it undermines the ethical and moral strength of all that America was built on.

I guess that Elites think by changing the mind-set of America's youth, they can alter the opinions and beliefs of future generations. Hitler tried to persuade the Nazi youth to hate and persecute Jews. We saw the result of his efforts.

Is preaching and teaching hate any less evil that restricting the positive values held by Christians? Do we wish to sit around and wait to see what a country without Christian values will look like? Elites believe that they, personally, are the highest power in the universe. There is no room for God in the minds of most of these individuals. Their behavior has given us a frightening preview of the corruption and chaos to come in an America without Christianity.

Without religion and without the morals that religion instills in all of us, society is destined to crumble. By continually pushing the limits of the actions and behavior that society deems acceptable, we continue to slide towards the precipice of societal decay.

Leaders of the new utopia will strive for a Godless society so society would no longer have right and wrong. Everything would be acceptable and any atrocities committed as a result of their amoral behavior would simply be accepted. The new society would have little need for authority or even law enforcement because no laws determining right from wrong will exist.

Again, to some small portion of the population this "No rules, no consequences" society would be their idea of the perfect world. This moral free-for-all; this do it if it feels good mentality; this desecration of America may be their idea of a perfect world. It's not mine!

# UTOPIA GOAL NUMBER 3
# GUN CONTROL….NO…. GUN BANS!

Ask any dictator what his thoughts on citizen's gun ownership rights are and he'll tell you that it's a crime punishable by severe prison sentences or worse. A gun in the hands of those he rules over is a threat to his power. The only people allowed to have power are the rulers. Likewise, if you asked a Liberal leader the same question he'd respond by saying that in a civilized and advanced society like ours, personally owned firearms were simply not needed. What they mean by that is, firearms give individuals power and only liberal leaders should have power.

Members of an armed society can stand up and defend themselves against cruelty, mistreatment and heavy-handed rulers. This is not acceptable in a society that is ruled over. It's been said that citizens have guns and that subjects have none. This is because without the ability to fight, you give up your ability to be free.

For the past several decades the Liberals who are trying to create utopia have been fighting to limit and ultimately ban gun ownership in the United States. Their rhetoric is deceptive and underhanded. Their scare tactics have been shameless. And somehow their strength has been growing. Playing on the fears of those not familiar and not comfortable around firearms, groups such as Hand Guns Inc., events like the Million-Mom March, and liberal leaders like Diane Feinstein, tout the dangers that guns present to our society. They give misleading statistics that show inflated numbers related to children injured or killed by firearms in America. They tell us that gun bans would save lives and prevent crime. They tell us guns are offensive to citizens and that anything that offends someone must be done away with. They want us to believe the armed forces and the government should be the only ones to have access to firearms. They see absolutely no purpose for guns in the hands of the citizens in today's society. They think even until now the only possible reason to own a gun was for hunting, but that is barbaric and is no longer an acceptable way to treat our fellow creatures. Remember, without guns citizens become subjects.

So in the new utopia all guns would be dutifully turned over the authorities to be destroyed by either melting them or cutting them into pieces. This would eliminate nearly all violent crime and make society a much, much safer place in which to live. Without guns the criminals would be unable to commit armed robbery, kidnappings, rape and murder. Thankfully all criminals dutifully turned their guns over to the authorities like the law-abiding citizens were forced to do. Now, with the guns out of the hand of the criminals, the good folks in society would have nothing to protect themselves from and therefore no use for guns.

To Liberals this seems to be very well thought out! In fact, it is so well thought out that now only the Utopia of the United States military and Utopias government leaders have access to firearms. Thank goodness the military can be trusted to the egomaniacal elitist leaders of the new utopia.

Imagine if the Jews that were being marched into Nazi death camps would have been armed citizens. Long before they'd be taken from their homes and shipped to their deaths, they would have stood up to Hitler and his hit men with force and bullets. A tragedy that is now in the history books could have been largely avoided or at the very least mitigated, if only they had the ability to fight for themselves.

To be able to manipulate and push people around without repercussions is far easier than persuading people through logic and respect. This is the reason that dictators will not allow the private ownership of firearms and this is why Liberals are trying to ban them at every turn today. How do you take the guns away from a free society? You lie.

Elites have no problem lying to the general public as long as they think the general public's best interests will be protected. It happened with the Clinton "Assault Weapons" bill. That bill banned guns that were cosmetically threatening to a group of Liberals who were not familiar with any of the guns included in the ban. The propaganda they spewed forth in an effort to pass the bill was nothing more than exaggerations, misinformation and down right lies. Again, Elites like Diane Feinstein, Ted Kennedy and John Kerry lied to the public in order to further their agenda of taking guns out of the hands of the American public. They know that we're to "Stupid" and stubborn to willingly relinquish our firearms so they lie and use scare tactics to frighten the public into believing that guns will undoubtedly kill their children. They tell us guns are the *cause* of violence in urban cities. Guns *make* gang members hate and kill each other. Guns *create* violence among American citizens. Liberals on Capitol Hill repeat these lies and many more regarding the evils of firearms. Eventually the media gets a hold of the misinformation and does it's very best to disseminate it. Sooner or later a lie that is told enough becomes the truth. The justification for them to panic, scare, lie and deceive us is, "It's in all of our best interest" to do away with those damn guns. The problem for gun owners is that the scare tactics used by gun-banning Liberals often work. There are thousands of Americans who are unfamiliar with firearms and their applications in the hands of law-abiding folks. Many might not have much of an opinion on gun ownership at all. Unfortunately there are more of these types of individuals than there are responsible gun owners. This is the segment of society that the Elites target for their scare campaigns. They twist and lie in order to convince neutral minded citizens that guns are the main reason for our social ills. They tell them there is little, if any reason, for Americans to own guns. The media repeats it and suddenly gun owners are in a daily fight for their constitutional rights.

What the Elites fail to realize is that the Second amendment is the reason the first amendment will forever be preserved. Or maybe they know this and are trying to eliminate the second amendment to eventually quiet all voices that question their agenda. It has worked well in other nations to disarm and then disenfranchise. Are the Elites just following suit?

Too much common sense makes the elites' heads hurt, so the next few sentences should be taken with three aspirin if you're a wacko left elitist Liberal:

If criminals no longer had access to firearms in order to intimidate and cause harm during the commission of a felony, don't you think they might look for the next most suited instrument for the job? Just because a criminal can't grab a 9mm from under his car seat doesn't mean he'll suddenly decide to give up crime and go straight. It's been proven in Europe and Australia that in fact, gun bans only insure that bad guys in society retain their weapons while the honest law-abiding citizens are left defenseless. Setting this fact aside let's assume for just a moment, that the bad guys would turn their weapons in alongside you and I. Then they too would be left without guns. Now let's try to think for the elites here. Can you think of anything other item a criminal might use as weapon in the commission of a crime? A couple of things come to mind that the elites seemed to have overlooked. A knife or a baseball bat would sure persuade me to turn over my wallet. I'd be willing to bet a liquor store owner would put up little resistance against a robber with a pitchfork. How persuasive could a carjacker be if he pressed an ice pick to your throat? Maybe a car could be used to murder somebody. I guess the elites will just have to work on the outlawing of farm tools, sports paraphernalia, automobiles and kitchen utensils. I'm sure they'll work on that just as soon as they've accomplished banning guns.

Some of the nations worst serial killers used guns in the commission of their crimes while others did not. Was Richard Ramirez a more evil or dangerous person as a result of using a gun in his crimes than John Wayne Gacy, who used other weapons? Gacy's body count was nearly three times as high as Ramirez' but Liberals would have you believe that evil guns and no other weapons, are the tools used by killers. It never crossed the minds of these intellectual giants that it is the act and not the weapon that results in the death of a killer's victim. It seems reasonable to me that anybody with the cognitive ability to reason, would come to the obvious and clichéd conclusion that "Guns don't kill people", any more than it's the hammers fault for hitting a nail or the cars fault for running into a tree. For a group of people who would like us to believe they're intellectually superior to us common folks, I'm confident the Elites lack the requisite knowledge and common sense to make *any* of my decisions for me.

Like any other tool used by man, guns are simply inanimate objects and like any other tool, they are not inherently good nor are they inherently evil. They are simply metal and plastic devises used for a variety of jobs and recreation. That's all! It's the person who uses the tool that determines whether it will be a danger or not.

If the goal of banning guns were really to reduce crime, then it would make sense to ban other weapons used by criminals to commit crimes, wouldn't it? Here's why that's not a big priority for the Left. Obviously a citizen with a knife is not a threat to the government. A group of farmers with hay-hooks can't overthrow an armed military. No real threat is posed to those in power by a couple of punks with a Louisville Slugger. It kind of makes me wonder about the reasons Liberals are so adamant about taking my guns away from me. How about you?

Beware of any group of people who want to infringe on any of you constitutional rights. They have a reason and an end goal for doing so. It is due to the foresight and brilliance of our founding fathers that, as citizens, we have the right to stand up against freedom-repressing Elites with force, if necessary. Take away our ability to stand and fight against those infringing on our rights and eventually we'll have no rights at all.

I digress, back to life in the perfect world. Sounds good doesn't it? A country free of guns and therefore free of crime. Be careful what you wish for, though. Here's a little Liberal "If...Then" logic for you. If it's decided that guns kill people, then it is reasonable to assume that misspelled words are the fault of my pencil. If so, banning guns would solve murder and banning pencils would eliminate misspelled words. Hey, I just solved the whole murder rate thing *and* fixed our nation's spelling problems!

# Utopia Goal Number 4
# Urban Consolidation

Ask any liberal politician what one of his main focuses is and you'll hear the word environment. There have been countless pieces of legislation introduced and passed into law that restrict you and I from enjoying Mother Nature. They have put restrictions on where we can camp, where we can ride horses, where we can fish and hunt. They even tell us how much we have to pay to enjoy our "Public" lands.

These are the first small steps to discourage you from getting out into the forests, deserts, mountains and prairies. They don't believe that you and I have any reason to disturb nature's delicate balance by enjoying what nature has to offer. Nor do they want anybody to live outside of their established urban boundaries. This includes those who currently live in the suburbs, on farmland, in the forests, on the prairies and in the mountains.

Going a step further, dreamy-eyed Liberals want to restore the country to the state it was before Europeans settled and developed its lands. They'd like to restore wetlands in the west where millions of tons of Alfalfa and oat & pea hay are now raised to sustain the nation's ranchers. Potato crops currently grown to offer Americans a food staple would be eliminated. They want to eliminate the corn and wheat fields in the vast Great Plains to restore prairie grass and buffalo herds. This means clearing people off of lands that simply "Don't need to be occupied." Liberals deem farmland, ranches, mills and rural factories unnecessary infringements on nature. For the past 40 years Liberals have been concocting ways to shut these land uses down and force rural residents to move to major cities. They've banned the logging industry from cutting down trees. They've shut water off to farmlands that will shrivel and die without it. They've closed rangeland to grazing cattle forcing ranchers to find alternate ways to feed their herds. They've put such strict emission standards on rural factories that they're forced to close or pay astronomical fines.

Liberals have started to systematically shut down America's lands by forcing roundabout regulations and injunctions. If a farmer can't farm and a logger cant' cut and a rancher can't ranch and a factory can't produce, where do these people go to find work to feed their families? They go to where the work is. In the cities and big towns where everyone else lives. Right where the Liberals want you so they can keep you off "Public" lands.

The reasoning behind their thinking is if all of the nation's population is in urban areas, the environmentalists can get to work on restoring each flower, each tree and each blade of grass to the condition it was in before we settled the country. Besides, isn't it easier to keep an eye on the cattle when they're pinned up together than it is when they're roaming freely on the open range?

It would be a huge surprise to metropolis-dwelling, card-carrying tree huggers that not all of the citizens of this country wish to live in such close proximity to one another. It would further confuse them to learn that having space and room to roam is a much sought after goal of Americans, going all the way back to the days when settlers explored the New World. These self-proclaimed "Protectors of Mother Earth" simply cannot comprehend why anybody would want to live in the mountains or on the prairie where their very existence is "Ruining" that particular ecosystem.

Somehow the eco-idealists find a niche in a world that they say should have no human interference. You and I are invaders and destroyers of the environment but these folks think they're just a tree in a forest or a blade of grass on a prairie. Unlike other humans, the eco-idealists would have us believe they don't use the oxygen supply by breathing. Apparently they don't eat, drink, or create bodily waste either. Those things would be considered to have a negative impact on the environment. They believe they're so in tune with the environment surrounding them, that they actually become "One" with it. They ask, "Why should farmers and ranchers be allowed on lands that are my brother and sister?" They truly believe the only way the environment can survive is if they can get all humans and non-native animals off the land that so desperately needs their protection.

We've heard the enviro-idealists tell us buildings and roads are smothering the earth, and people need to be moved off the lands of this precious treasure called earth. Aside from genocide, the only solution to saving the planet is to consolidate all humans into huge urban cities where they can do little damage to land outside the metropolis in which they exist. Having us cooped up and off the land is the goal of eco-idealists. They've already set the proverbial wheels in motion. Land buy-outs, water shut-offs, wetland restoration and special interest groups like the Sierra Club and the Earth Liberation Front, are all doing their part to consolidate this country's population into urban areas. This is urban consolidation. This is rural cleansing.

The new utopia would consist of miles and miles of vertical living. One family camped above and below other families. Can you imagine the quantity of apartment units needed to accommodate each and every rural citizen of this country? The thought of high-rises encompassing entire cities does nothing for me. Every city in the country would be a New York or a Los Angeles. There would be no "Quaint" little towns. There would be no suburbs. Everything would be concentrated into the smallest area necessary to house and contain our population. The thought of driving on streets where twenty million others are trying to drive at the same time brings the term "Road-rage" to mind. The crime rate and stress level would be sky-high as a result of cramming such a huge number of people into such a close and confined living space. Think of the health issues that would affect a population forced to live in such close proximity. A single case of the flu could easily shut down an entire city within a week. Anything as deadly as SARS could wipe out a fair share of the population. Infection rates of air born viruses would be around 100%. Sounds like utopia to me.

Employment opportunities associated with rural cleansing would be extremely limited. This would force fierce competition among those competing for the relatively few jobs that would be available. With all farmers, ranchers and timber industry workers bottled up in urban hell, millions of people in jobs related to rural life would be instantly unemployed. The government of our new utopia would have to find a way to subsidize those who were forced out of work and into the sixty-percent unemployment rate. In the name of the environment, urban consolidation would reduce our GDP to a fraction of what it is now and render the United Utopian States of America (UUSA) impotent to compete in a world market.

I wonder if those who preach urban consolidation ever considered how concentrating the entire country's population into a few huge mega-cities would effect the environment. Pollution and waste would be extremely concentrated. We would literally live amongst our refuse disposal sites. Air quality would be so poor that the elderly and infirm would be in physical danger each time they stepped outside. Any body of water surrounding these super cities would be cesspools of contamination and urban seepage. Are we to assume that these conditions are a necessary evil to preserve ninety-nine percent of the land in America? Have they decided that a few places of extremely concentrated pollution is better for the environment that many small pockets of it scattered across the nation? What will become of the endangered worm or butterfly that exist only in the region where the Elites plan their super-cities? I'm sure they'll justify the extinction of a few species to save others throughout the country, just like they are now willing to justify sacrificing relatively few farmers and ranchers to save millions of poor innocent fish throughout the nation. I truly believe that the enviro-idealists need to revisit their high school science courses that cover the chapter on natural selection and adaptation.

We are wicked and evil people for using the gifts mother earth offers. Earth's human inhabitants are "exploiting" oil, water, trees and even oxygen. Is it evil for us to produce corn, wheat, fruit, vegetables, beef and thousands of other foodstuffs that feed the nation? Referred to as "Rapers of Mother Earth" by the more extreme environmentalists, farmers have kept this country supplied with all the life-sustaining food products needed to keep our country food-independent. Raising crops and cattle may benefit the ongoing survival of mankind but surely it's not worth the impact on the environment it causes. In fact, the greenies might wish to think twice about where there next vegetarian meal would come from. If all of the farmers were now in the big city and no land could be used for non-native vegetation, there would be a sudden panic among non-meat eaters across the country. The sheer number of acres required to produce fruits and vegetables is astounding.

If every citizen of the UUSA were forced, by lack of choice, to be a vegetarian, our now empty farmlands and orchards would be inert and incapable of being used for growing. With the short shelf life of most produce, importation and distribution of fruits and vegetables to the citizens of the new utopia would be nearly impossible.

Compounding the problem is the fact that these bunny-huggers eat only organic produce and the use of pesticides or preservatives are strictly taboo.

To environmentalists who live in the bubble of peace and tranquility, urban consolidation seems like the end-all cure-all solution to earth's problems. Little do they know that it would be the ruin of our nation and destruction of our society. Greenies wouldn't even be alive if weren't for the contributions made by America's rural inhabitants. When you think about the flawed thought process and lack of common sense among Liberals, it makes me wonder if Darwin's "Natural selection" is actually working the way he theorized it would. If it did, I'm convinced that Liberals would be extinct by now.

We might not be able to feed the citizens of the new utopia but thanks to urban consolidation and rural cleansing, at least the land would be as pristine as it was three hundred years ago. That's just the way a perfect world should be to some. Not to me!

# Utopia Goal Number 5
# Environmental Perfection!

## Timber Cutting Bans

Ahhh…imagine all the trees in the forest. Healthy, tall, strong, hundreds of years old and as thick as the hair on a dog's back. Think of the underbrush that provides the ecosystem for forest critters large and small. The forest looks so good and is so "Healthy" because environmentalists have blocked all logging in this forest. Not one tree has been cut in nearly twenty years. None of the natural underbrush that provides shelter for grubs and finches has been cleared. This forest is a role model for what environmentalists want every forest in the country to be like. This will show the damn timber industry (who wants nothing more than to get rich by destroying all forests) what all future forests will look like.

Now imagine a late September thunderstorm crossing the peaks of the mountain range and settling into the valley. Thunder claps as lightning strikes the dry forest floor and ignites a fire. Now all the underbrush and dangerously thick timber create a catastrophic fire that burns so hot and so furiously that firefighters can't fight it. The fire claims everything in its path. Old growth forests, timber that environmentalists fall over themselves to protect, burns to the ground. Wildlife, including endangered owls, wolverines and the blue-toed three-eyed salamander all perish, alongside the common deer, skunk, rabbit and bear. Watersheds are destroyed due to soil erosion following the fire. The fisheries are ruined and native trout and steelhead die and become endangered as a result.

Now *that's* a good forest preservation plan if I've ever heard one. Of course it has destroyed the very forest that the plan was intended to protect, but that's beside the point. The point is that loggers and the timber industry have been put out of business due to logging bans. Timber that loggers claimed, "Needed to be thinned" to prevent uncontrollable forest fires, wasn't murdered by greedy timber companies. The clearing of years upon years of underbrush would have destroyed the nests of finches and upset the soil where the Western Grub frolics. Thanks to protests, injunctions, green demonstrations and activist judges, the underbrush was protected and bug's lives were temporarily spared.

The problem with these eco-idealists who dedicate their lives to protecting the forest, is that they have no clue as to what a healthy forest is. Their idea of a healthy forest is an untouched forest, when that is simply not the case. The thinning of overgrown timber and the clearing of underbrush are essential tools in maintaining a clean and healthy forest. It obviously benefits in the reduction of fuel when a fire does start. Still, the eco-idealists see these measures as destructive and invasive to the forest and it's residents.

In the new utopia every judge will be an activist judge. All requests by environmental groups to halt timber sales will be granted and injunctions will be put on other sales, eventually denying all logging of public and private lands. It will be in the new utopia that millions of dollars in research funds will be spent on the development of wood-alternative products. These new products made of plastic, recycled glass, soy bean boards, compressed Lilly pads or whatever, will take the place of all wood products so no tree is sacrificed for the comfort or convenience of the invaders that the environmentalists call humans.

Think of the dignity that could be returned to trees if their products were no longer used as toiler paper, copy paper, paper towels, books, calendars, newspapers, documents, cardboard boxes, or adding machine tape. Trees would celebrate the day dimensional lumber was banned from stores. No longer could you go to the lumberyard and buy any kind of lumber. Happy days indeed for environmentalists who have spent countless nights sleeping in trees and endless days chained to logging equipment. Mission accomplished!

Loggers, mill workers, retailers and all other timber-related workers would be ostracized in the new utopia and seen as murderous brutes. With little chance of rehabilitation in their own communities, the former timber-slaughterers would be forced to move to new towns where their past was unknown. In a new town amongst strangers, just maybe, they could be retrained for a respectable profession.

As a way to minimize the amount of human started fires in the wonderfully thick forests, the law will strictly enforce a "Keep the public off public lands" policy that will in essence ban all non-government persons from being in the Nations Forests. Only with the express written consent of the Utopia Forest Service (U.F.S.), and after careful consideration of the Forest Safety Board will permits for restricted use be issued to individuals or groups. Additional safety measures will be taken to insure forest safety. Thousands of jobs will be created in the "Keep the Forests Wet" campaign. This system of forest-wide sprinklers will stop all fires shortly after they start. A non-invasive system of nearly invisible and ultra non-toxic organic sprinkler pipes will be laid throughout the forest floor by countless government workers to protect each and every tree from the dangers of fire. With any luck, scientists in the new utopia will find a way to force thunderclouds to dissipate before they reach the point of lightning and thunder. This would insure safe forests and would make those annoying destructive storms of light a thing of the past. After all, they serve no purpose and we don't need them.

Just before the total extinction of every tree here in the U.S., the liberal enviro-idealists have saved the day. Another job well done to save us from ourselves here in the perfect world.

## Save the Fish

Here in the west we've seen our share of conflicts between farmers and environmentalists. Between fisherman and environmentalists. Between the commercial fishing industry and environmentalists. Between ranchers and environmentalists. Between hydro-electric energy producers and environmentalists. Do you start to see a pattern with the antagonist character in all of these scenarios? Environmentalists usually claim that the continued existence of a little known fish or newly discovered tadpole are the primary reason to shut off water to farms or to stop fishermen from invading the habitat of a certain river species of minnow.

We've learned that Environmentalists will pursue ridiculous legal battles to the bitter end, regardless of the animal whose very existence is at stake. Regardless of what needs to be done to preserve water quality for the insects who supply a food source to the endangered species of fish. Regardless of the results of their beloved Environmental Impact Studies, they pursue their idealistic goals instead of listening to logic and reason.

In my home state of Oregon, a corporation intended to build a small ski resort to provide entertainment to residents of our rural county. After exhaustive environmental impact studies and numerous rulings by activist judges, the discovery of evidence proving the existence of wolverines on the very mountain where the resort was to be built, was discovered. Thought to be non-existent in our state for decades, wolverines were here again and must be considered endangered. After further studies by outside sources, it became apparent that employees of the Forest Service, who did not want to see the resort become a reality, were planting the evidence that "proved" the wolverine's existence here. Another example of how the Elite knows better than we do, what is best for us.

Fish, in other parts of the state and throughout the country, have become the wolverine of my town. Farmers have had their water completely shut off and their entire crop season lost, so the water level of a lake that supports the Short-Nosed Suckerfish could be maintained. This lake is 26 miles long and one of the largest bodies of water in the Northwest, but in an effort to progress the agenda of rural cleansing, the environmentalists bravely stood up for the fish's water rights. In a veiled effort to force farmers and ranchers to leave their land, the enviro-idealists ruined millions of dollars in crops, bankrupt small and large farms alike, and forced more than one family to sell out and move off their land. All in the name of the Suckerfish.

This was a real eye-opener for many in rural communities across the country. We all learned to what extremes these environmental wacko's were willing to go to progress their agenda.

To deny ranchers and farmers water rights, elitist judges who think ranching and farming is stupid, have ruled to shut down water to these individuals thus attempting to eliminate their way of life. If they can promote downstream flows of water in western rivers by listing the Coho salmon as an endangered species, they can redirect the water intended for farmers and ranchers, to the rivers that promote these poor fish who thrive in the west.

Since the fish already seem to be the key to rural cleansing, the new utopia will preserve the rights of wild fish in streams and oceans, rivers and lakes. Recreational fishing will be pronounced cruel and dangerous to the future of all species of sport fish. Commercial fishing will grind to a halt due to even more limiting seasons, severe restrictions and fees. The harvest of shellfish and tuna will stop. The only food application fish we'll have is in the fish farms developed for food raising purposes. Aqua-farms will be strictly monitored if not government-run and will raise sufficient amounts of fish to feed the leaders of our new utopia and any visiting foreign dignitaries. The ultra rich will be allowed to bid for fish in occasional auctions that sell surplus stock.

Exceptions will be made for minority groups who use fish in ceremonies. These will include various Native American groups as well as Eskimos. Due to their delicate existence they will be given full exemption from all laws governing the harvest of wild fish in the new utopia. Other groups who reference fish as part of their religious history, such as the Christians, will be shown no leniency in the laws governing the harvest of wild fish. After all, it's the damn Christian's fault that the fish are in such drastic trouble today.

A perfect world for those who consider fishing "Cruelty to animals." Perfect for those who don't eat fish and don't think others should. Perfect for you? Certainly not for me.

## No Drilling

The infallible leaders of our new and improved....no, perfect world, will promptly do away with any and all drilling by companies, corporations and individuals. No drilling for oil, gas, water, or even maple syrup will be tolerated. In fact, just the ownership of drills, augers, bits, chucks, or any other drilling paraphernalia by individuals or corporations will be strictly prohibited.

In the new utopia all will be well in the environment, if not for those who inhabit it. This is as it should be. Already, greenies are angry with you and me, the government and everyone who has ever done anything that could be remotely considered harmful to the environment.

Even the word "Natural" gas should indicate to everyone with half a brain that it is automatically off limits to use and exploitation. As we know, there is no way to tap into natural gas reserves without penetrating and violating Mother Earth. Sound dirty? You bet it is! It's the rape of the natural world and the utter destruction of the planet.

Due to the invasive nature of obtaining natural gas, it's use for heating and cooking purposes is not only selfish but also compromises the ecosystem, world-wide. It's only sensible then that the government of the new utopia will deem natural gas a national treasure and will outlaw its development and use.

Oil is to the greenies as sugar is to your gas tank. It should go without saying that oil drilling, refining and use would be halted immediately in the new utopia. It *should* go without saying, but it would be the biggest enviro-whacko accomplishment the world has ever seen. Celebrations by hippies and tree huggers would stretch from boarder to boarder and coast to coast.

Following the outlawing of fossil fuels, the oil pipelines that stretch from Alaska to the mainland would be shut down and disassembled. The materials used in the pipeline would be recycled into environmentally friendly building materials. The oil derricks in the costal waters off California and in the Gulf of Mexico would be given the cease and desist order and would be shut down and towed back to shore, retired forever. The oilfields of Oklahoma, Texas and Wyoming would be systematically shut down and towns around them would be as empty as the gas tank of your car. And speaking of cars, there would be no automobiles on the roads, thus achieving a long-stated goal of the far left. Airports around the country would be deserted as no flights would be departing and all flights entering the new utopias boarders would be diverted to further reduce pollution.

As a result of us nasty Americans not being allowed to drill for fuel sources, a person in the new utopia could almost see with their bare eyes, the hole in the ozone closing. Within a week or two all signs of global warming would disappear and the melting of polar ice caps would cease. Within six months, species that were thought to be extinct would magically reappear in utopias heartland giving bug lovers and bunny huggers more cause for celebration. Yes, without the evils of oil and the resulting pollution, the new utopia would be the perfect role model for less advanced societies around the world.

The resulting effects of not having any vehicular transportation except bicycles and skateboards would be deemed a necessary sacrifice in the fight to save the planet. Businesses employing workers that commute to and from work would be asked by utopian officials to postpone business and commerce until alternate means of long distance transportation could be developed.

As they usually do, the Elites will have put the cart before the horse. Only now would liberal leaders authorize and provide funding for the development of alternative fuel vehicles. Research and development would be funded by your tax dollars and would require a raise in your taxes to expedite the implementation of the new technology.

This tax raise would be hard on those who are out of work because they are not allowed to use transportation to their place of work, but we would all be expected to accept this as a necessary sacrifice. Until those vehicles are developed and we can all get back to work, it's just good enough that the planet is beginning to heal itself.

With oil and natural gas a thing of the past, the environmentalists can focus on the abuses being perpetrated on the nations water. Aside from its use in metropolitan areas by the residents of high rises and a million apartments, water should be listed as a an "Endangered natural resource." This would provide it protection against well drilling by the holdouts in rural areas that have still not relocated to the big cities of the new utopia. Any remaining farmlands would be denied any and all water rights under the new "Water Protection Act" appointed into law by one of many liberal activist judges. All man-made dams across the country would be removed to return water's habitat to its natural state. The sacrifice of electrical power provided by hydroelectric dams would be a small price to pay to insure that water is once again frolicking in its natural state.

The message, and ensuing new legislation, in the utopia-to-be is that there is no excuse for humans to exploit any of the life-sustaining natural resources in this country just for the benefit of mankind. When misguided misfits control policy concerning the well being of America's citizens and that of the land we live on, we are in serious trouble.

Yes, an earth without holes in it is a happy earth indeed. This is another aspect of the environmentalist's perfect world. Personally, I'd rather being driving to work in my SUV drinking bottled water from a well at Mt. Shasta. How about you?

# UTOPIA GOAL NUMBER 6
## EDUCATIONAL REFORM

The school system in the new utopia would be barely recognizable to students in today's primitive and crude educational system. The future will prove to be a much more student-friendly place to learn.

In the reform of the school system, the first thing to go would be the issuance of letter grades to mark a students achievements and progress. This archaic system of determining a student's progress and understanding of a given subject by issuing a letter grade is demeaning and can be potentially damaging to the psyche of a child. Doesn't it seem amazing that the paddle-toting, ruler slapping educators of the past were allowed to not only issue letter grades but also command the attention of students and even discipline them when they were disruptive or rude? How far we will have come when the new educational system is in place.

Schools in the new utopia would evaluate their students on how well a student could recite the instructor's beliefs. Students would also be evaluated on the basis of how well they believed they were doing in a given class. A student who says, "I feel like I'm doing great in social studies" would translate to an automatic A, or the new equivalent there of. All students would pass every course with honors because

not to do so just might make a student feel bad about him/
herself. To stifle a student by requiring such traditional
and rigid instruction would be cruel. New utopian math
would be based on how a student felt about numbers and
their interpretations of equations. If a student were to think
that 2+2=5 or 3x4=Cat, then it's that's students right and
*no* teacher has the right to tell student's their thoughts are
wrong. This progressive teaching is incredibly helpful in the
building of confidence in young students. It would push our
nations grade point average high enough that our children
could finally compete with the averages of children learning
in other nations.

Equally repressive is the attention to detail that
traditional teachers put on proper spelling. Red markers
that are currently used to point out mistakes on student's
papers will be banned from the classroom. In fact, this has
already happened in a few school districts across the country.
It has been determined by today's child psychologists that
the red marks on a student's paper make that child feel as
if he/she has made a mistake. As crude and insensitive as it
may seem, when a student was required to write a story or do
a report in the "old" system, teachers used to grade a student
on grammar, spelling, punctuation *and* content.

When a student made a mistake red marks did indeed
point out their errors. This produced a literate individual at
the end of a school career. As demanding as this sounds, it's
true. I guess none of us knew the red marks on our papers
were damaging our psyche. Teachers in the new educational
system will be trained to ignore the less important aspects
of the written language in order to preserve a student's self-
perception and dignity.

Content, not spelling or grammar will be considered in
the evaluation of a student's work. Spelling is not important
if the actual requirement to spell correctly interferes with a
student's ability to put their imagination on paper. Soon, any

color of marker used for correcting papers, (which makes students feel like they've made a mistake) will be removed from the classroom. Mistakes should not be pointed out so discreetly. This includes those highly overemphasized spelling errors. BEsides its noT impotent thet KiDs spel corectally iF there Good studints!

Not only would the new system ease up on the demanding and restrictive curriculum, it would shorten the amount of time a student spends in a containing and physically restrictive classroom. As it is, the hours required of a student are just too physically taxing. The formerly rigid schedule of school starting at 8:00am would be banished. Adolescents and teens should not be forced to awake in the morning before their biological clocks wake them on their own. School hours will also be shortened in the afternoon to allow more "Personal time" for students. Educators in the new system will be made aware of the importance and need for young folks to develop good playing skills. School should not interfere with this more than absolutely necessary. Besides, a start time so early requires a student to go to bed earlier than he may want to. It requires the student to get up in the morning before he has obtained the required 12-14 hours of sleep that teens think they need. Early start times require a student to perform such complicated tasks of dressing and eating breakfast before they are fully awake and ready to do such things. This is obviously far too much strain to put on our youth. How educators in the past could expect so much from kids so young is simply appalling. It's no wonder with the issuance of grades, set start times and required correct answers, that so many students in the old school system had difficulty once in a while and didn't find school their favorite place to be. It's a miracle that not every single one of them had low self-esteem issues or severe depression.

The school calendar will also look different in the new utopia. The current amount of time students get out of school for holidays, teacher in-service days, grading preparation days, half days and late start days, simply isn't enough. To ensure the optimal learning capabilities of students, our new educators will be sure their minds are plenty rested. To create a better learning environment the new schools will have late start every Monday as the weekend can be draining on young people. This will allow for tired students to get caught up on the sleep they missed during their busy weekend. It will also allow them to spend the rest of their shortened school day learning at optimum levels.

Every Friday will be an early dismissal day for students in America. Limiting days off to just Saturday, Sunday and half of Monday is simply too restrictive. This will allow youngsters extra time to play and plan their busy days off before the weekend actually starts.

Holiday breaks don't allow for enough time before and after the actual holiday for students to first prepare for celebration and then afterwards, recover from the festivities. To fix this problem, the month before and the month following major holidays, will be given off to America's students. This will allow them to fully concentrate on school before the excitement of the Holiday draws too near. It will also allow for the full emotional recovery of students before returning to school, following the big celebration. Summer break should be just that. The new utopia won't think of convening school before sweaters are required to fend off the chill of cooler temperatures in late summer or most likely, early fall. Likewise, School will adjourn for summer at the first sign of t-shirt weather. This allows students a full recuperative break from three or four grueling months of instruction.

Also important to the new system will be a "Learn-at-your-own-pace" policy that will allow all students to progress through the school system at a pace that is comfortable for them. After all, we're not all clones and therefore require drastically different amounts of time to comprehend ideas, theories and to interpret facts. There will be no shame in a twenty-seven year old student struggling to complete the ninth grade. Nor will any judgment be passed on a seven year old with three college degrees, as long as he felt he's earned them.

Thankfully, for the emotional and psychological welfare of the nation's students-to-be, all of these issues will be addressed and remedied in the new utopia. No stress learning environments and ultra low-pressure curriculums promote happy students and isn't that the goal the new system is striving to achieve?

Speaking of a change in curriculum, there will be a new and intriguing course that will be required learning for any and all students. The new utopia's "Revamped and Updated History of the United States" would be tantamount in the system's curriculum. This course will correct all perceived wrongdoings that the less advanced and far less progressive former establishment purveyed on people and policies here and abroad.

Let's open the first chapter of the schools new history book, shall we? The new history book will tell our students of how integration and diversity were the key reasons for the importation of people from Africa in the seventeenth and eighteenth centuries. How these noble people were eager and willing to voyage to the new world where they were admired for their religion and were encouraged to share their cultural and societal traditions and ways of life.

The new history book will remind us how Black and White children played together at community picnics and social events where all were welcome and eventually grew up to be interracial couples living atop seventeenth century society. And that's the way it really was, kids!

43

The concept of "Boot strap mentality" will be set straight as well. How cruel and insensitive for a civil society to expect one to better himself by working hard, being disciplined and advancing through determination and success. The new history book will explain how, since the beginning of time, there have been social programs for those in society who just didn't feel like getting out there and supporting themselves. It will tell the heartwarming story of how Abraham Lincoln had help from the good folks of the Illinois chapter of Habitat For Humanity in building his historic log cabin. How craftsmen donated the hand-cut dimensional lumber needed for the floors and roof because old Abe just didn't have the time to cut his own lumber. Then as the cabin neared completion the crew from Monster Cabin Makeover swarmed Abe's property to plant trees, lawns and complete the landscape design. Yes indeed, it was a wonderful time in our nations history. It demonstrates how one can benefit from the hard work of others.

The new history book will teach our children of the time when Thomas Jefferson commissioned a journey for Lewis and Clark to travel westward to document and report on their discoveries. It will tell of the importance of the food stamps, which he persuaded the government to issue to members of the expedition. The purpose being, that on days when discovery was vital to westward expansion, it would not always be convenient for these explorers to drop what they were doing to hunt, fish, or forage for their own food. The use of food stamps was imperative to the expedition by freeing up countless hours of time that was better used exploring and documenting all of the wondrous things of the west. There was also a strict "Leave No Footprint" policy put in place prior to their journey westward. Agreed to and signed by both the government and the members of the exploratory party, regulations to pick up all waste produced by the party's members and livestock was implemented.

Another mandate prohibited the party's members from cutting any trees for the purpose of shelter, transportation, or fire. As a stipulation of receiving the aforementioned food stamps, the killing of wild animals along the journey was deemed illegal as well. In the end, the explorers were able to cross the continent and stay the winter in Fort Clatsop, Oregon Territory. They did so without the use of a single branch of wood and with plenty of food stamps to see them home in the coming spring. These were the first real travelers to explore the reaches of the far west while truly living off the land.

As we read on in our new history book, the children of the new utopia will discover the differences made by the Industrial Revolution. How cotton gins and improved engines made production of everything from clothes to steel quicker and more efficient. How these wondrous machines were powered by the discovery and development of solar power and utilized hydrogen fueled engines.

Never in the modernization of our country did its population endanger air quality with the use of such crude fuels as coal or petroleum products. Yes, we were a more enlightened society then and with hard work we can return to that level of environmental prudence once again.

It will also be made perfectly clear to students of the new history that all inventions that helped to form the new world were gifts from the brilliant minds from our friends in France. Without France's inventors working hard to help us modernize, we would still be a country of primitive technology. We owe France our eternal gratitude and devotion for their kindness.

The new history book will paint the picture of a world that has known no conflict. In this depiction of lasting peace, our children will learn that we have always been in total agreement with nations around the world, especially the European nations with whom we've never had a disagreement. The history book reads, "Any of you who have heard of a thing called the Cold War, be assured that it was nothing more that the rumblings of a long-extinct human tribe called the Republicans." And with that, world peace can continue.

Now our children will have been "taught" everything the Liberals believe they need to know. The fact that little, if any of the history they've been taught is actually factual is unimportant. What matters is that these kids are open and willing to accept anything the Left decides is necessary for them to know. Apparently Liberals don't feel that future generations of children need educational skills like arithmetic, grammar, or history. It leads me to ask the question, "What kind of world do Elites envision where basic education is not considered important?" Do they really think with the new, more sensitive educational system in place, we can once again strive to make our country competitive and compliant with other nations around the world? It's just *another* thing the Left is doing that makes you say, "Wow!"

# UTOPIA GOAL NUMBER 7
## SPECIAL RIGHTS FOR MINORITY GROUPS

To hell with power in numbers and majority rules ideology. These bigoted and obsolete ideas will have no place in the new utopia. Special rights will rule the PC landscape.

Lets pretend that 100 people gather to watch a sporting event. We'll assume ninety-nine percent will want to watch football while one percent, in this case just 1 person, wishes to watch soccer. The way it used to be, majority would rule and football would be on the big screen. In the world of utopia, the one guy who wants to watch soccer will request a judge to consider the fact that he feels like he's outnumbered and that football offends his peaceful nature. That would be all the argument the judge would need to rule in favor of the one percent. We cannot have citizens running around feeling outnumbered or offended. Not only would "Soccer guy" win, the ninety-nine percent who voted for football would be forced to watch the soccer game as a form of punishment. This is fair to the minority in the new utopia. Maybe not fair to the other ninety-nine percent of us, but fair to them.

Lets look at gay folks in today's society. As recently as the early eighties, gay men and women in America stayed "In the closet," out of public view and away from public scrutiny. The "Don't ask, don't tell" policy was implemented in our military to keep homosexuals under wraps. We'd never heard of the term gay marriage, life partners, or gay communities. Back then, a guy and a girl got together, married, settled down had kids and enjoyed life as a family. In today's far more accepting world (see frog in warm water analogy) homosexuals are being allowed to trivialize such traditional concepts as marriage and family. Guy's want to marry guy's and girl's want to marry girls and they want me to be understanding of their feelings. They want to be able to walk hand-in-hand down the street or in the mall and not have anybody stare at them or comment or explain to our children why two men have their tongues in each other's mouths. Today, Elites want to teach our kids about "Alternative lifestyles" and "Diversity" and "Acceptance" instead of explaining right and wrong, the definition of debauchery, and pointing out any example of immoral or sinful behavior.

If gay's and their advocates have thus trivialized and already weakened the traditional idea of relationships, marriage and family, just imagine what things will be like in the new utopia. I can easily imagine entire cities and maybe even counties designated as gay communities where you must be a card-carrying homosexual to buy or rent a home. These would be the most scenic and desirable towns in the nation because to stick homosexual communities in less than ideal cities would be considered blatant discrimination. Because homosexuals would be considered as normal and morally equivalent to you and I, they would share all of the rights we have and enjoy others rights we don't have as regular straight people.

They could very well set up gay only election districts and stipulate that anybody running or voting in a particular district would have to prove he or she were gay. Cities, counties and then states could be gay run places that lean heavily towards gay-related issues and ignore much of the rest of the people in their region.

To see how the acceptance of the gay lifestyle is already being pushed on us just turn on your television. Go ahead, turn on your television today and try to find a design show, a home improvement show, or a sit-com that doesn't glorify queers in our society. Home improvement shows always have the gratuitous gay guy in their cast of four or five. He's the little fellow who talks with a lisp and works with fabrics instead of power tools. Hollywood has found a place for gays in many of its big screen productions. The design industry has been a Mecca for free spirited and sexually confused folks for years. In an effort to normalize homosexual behavior and to lessen the offense taken by their actions, we as Americans have been conditioned to be acceptant. By telling us that it's not a gay person's fault that they're gay and by telling us that their sexuality is genetic, we are made to feel sorry for gays. By broadcasting their lifestyles on TV and in movies the elites try to make the sight of gays normal. By telling us we're homophobic, the elites try to shame us into accepting the lifestyles and practices of our gay neighbors.

It is easy to imagine even more gay-friendly concepts in the not so distant future. As if there aren't enough choices on TV today, your family will have new choices in television programming. But if there is programming that targets families, then there damn well better be programming that caters to the entertainment of gays and lesbians. I can already imagine the launch of the Ellen DeGeneres owned, "All Queer, All Year" network that will be broadcast throughout the country. It's lineup of "All Gay, All Day" programming will cater to the lifestyles, humor and interests of gay citizens in the new utopia. Gay fashion, gay love stories, gay how-to shows and gay shows that I can't yet imagine, will be televised for all to watch. It will soon be as normal to turn on "Gay T.V." as it is to currently turn on Cartoon Network or Women's Entertainment. With any luck at all, we'll see the whole idea blossom and we'll be able to expect stations that cater to gay Black men between 18 and 40 years old or to White lesbians with a pet fetish.

It is obvious that the gay population in this country has been recognized. They've fought for and won special rights to be recognized by states as couples and by insurance companies as "Domestic partners."

Another way that Elites can use gays to further deconstruct our society is by giving gay couples the right to adopt children. We're told that gays can be, "Caring loving, compassionate parents" to children. With the shortage of children to fill the homes of infertile straight couples, the gays must have the Elites and activist judges pulling for them. Why else would a government agency place a small influential child in the home of a sexually confused deviate?

Society is curious as to why our children have so many behavioral problems and ask what can be done to return to the more traditional child raising techniques. Then we watch the news and hear stories of gay couples being granted adoption rights by a judge in some liberal metropolis like San Francisco or New York. We turn on the TV and see Rosie O'Donnell and her "Life Partner" or "Wife" being interviewed about their adoptive children and their happy family. These children grow up with the emotional conflict of having two parents of the same sex showing affection and having sex under the same roof. No judge or enlightened Elite can tell me *that* is a good environment for a small child. If Elites are allowed to continue to corrupt young minds by forcing the acceptance of homosexual behavior, our future generations have a slim chance of returning to anything resembling traditional values.

The gays have a strong foothold and an important role to play in the deconstruction of the United States. They are riding atop the wave of special rights and will undoubtedly be entitled to additional privileges in the near future. What a wonderful world awaits homosexuals in the new utopia to come.

I know there will be readers who gasp and say, "This guy's a real homophobe!" Actually, I remember a time before the word "homophobe" existed. I remember a time when all of this gay acceptance crap hadn't yet been forced down our throats. Political correctness dictates that I don't act offended by the actions of gays. It dictates that anyone not totally acceptant of the gay lifestyle is a homophobe. It dictates that being intolerant of the teaching of the homosexual lifestyle to my kids in school is bigoted and rude. Yet I remember a time before the term "Politically correct" was even thought of. I don't dislike gays any more than I dislike other members of our society who act immorally. I don't like criminals, liars, killers, or cheats. Yet I've never been referred to as a "Cheatophobe" or a "Criminophobe." I guess if these terms existed I would automatically be classified as both!

Special rights are important to the rebuilding of the new utopian society that the Elites are desperately trying to design. Actually, they're just as important to the destruction of the society in which we now live. By transforming America as a whole nation, into separate groups with separate rights, the elites are employing the divide and conquer strategy. Once broken down, a new society will take shape and Elites will be relentless in shaping it into the utopia they've always imagined.

Hiring policies are another example of giving minorities special rights. The equal opportunity folks have accomplished the passing and implementation of these policies and laws over the years. Luckily for the uneducated and unmotivated people of minority ethnic backgrounds, work is available to them. This is not because they are qualified to do the job they're given, but because the company who hires them has to meet ethnic and gender quotas.

When the qualifications for being hired are based on skin color or gender instead of education, experience or ability, then were back to full blown discrimination. To those who benefit from these new policies it's considered "positive" discrimination. Those non-minority job seekers who are passed up for employment are told they are more able to get work than a Korean man or a Black woman. Although the minorities that are given these jobs are frequently less qualified than their "Majority" counterparts, they start at the same or possibly higher wages than our "Majority" applicant would.

Several corporations are requiring a percentage of management positions be issued to women. These are not positions that are fought for by the two or three most qualified and experienced employees. Instead they are doled out like treats to a well-behaved pet simply based on gender.

With many government jobs, there are so many restrictions on who a supervisor may hire based on age, race, sexual preference and religious beliefs that you and I have little chance of ever being employed by a government agency. I have a friend whose son is a junior in college. He's changing his major from environmental studies to communications because he realized his desired major would do little to get him a job with the United States Forest Service. He told me at a get together a few weeks ago that if he were a fifty five year old Black lesbian woman who had six children and was on welfare, that he could probably have been hired without a problem. While this may seem a bit exaggerated right now, in the new utopia these characteristics may be actual requirements.

This is not to say that white males are the only qualified people for a given job. There are plenty of well-educated, equally qualified women and minorities in the workplace today. They work hard, pay taxes and make a living like any other American. My point here is that qualifications and education should be taken into consideration regardless of a person's ethnicity or gender.

The same preference is given to minority students when universities consider scholarships and financial aid. If a $10,000 scholarship is up for grabs and there are three students competing for it, there would be requirements that the applicants would have to meet. Applicant one is a White male with a 3.8 grade point average who is involved with school government and participates in school sports. Applicant number two is a White female who has a 4.0 grade point average. She volunteers at the local hospital and is involved with the school band. Applicant number three is a female Lebanese immigrant who has a 3.0 grade point average and has no extracurricular involvement. She has difficulty speaking English and has had attendance problems in the past. Who is the most qualified applicant?

Well that poor Lebanese girl deserves the scholarship because she's really struggling. Also, the university has just eighteen Lebanese students and has been encouraged to increase enrollment of all minorities. So, applicants one and two who have spent their high school careers striving to do their best, get involved, and meet scholarship qualifications are passed up to promote the advancement of a minority student who only did fair in high school. What encouragement does this give to "majority" kids to work a little extra or study a little longer if, when their chance for a scholarship arrives, it's given to a student who has done nothing right but be born in a foreign country? What message does it send to minority students? You will be given a scholarship if you wish to attend college even if you did nothing to earn the scholarship in high school. That does nothing to motivate these minority students to better themselves.

Do you think this causes a riff between white students and their minority counterparts in the nations universities?

Do you think it separates this group from that group more than ethnicity alone would have in the first place? Sure it does. Even "Positive discrimination" is only positive to one side of an issue. The other side is denied what used to be their right to equal consideration simply because there native to this country or because they have white skin.

The NAACP gets a huge charge out of hearing people like me talk about the issue of unfair consideration. It never fails that when this is brought up in discussion form on a news talk show, an NAACP spokesperson brings up injustices of a hundred and fifty years ago or the educational opportunities provided to Blacks sixty years ago. They see this practice of reverse discrimination as justice when they constantly preach to stop discrimination in this country. What they really want is the advancement of Blacks at the expense of Whites instead of the advancement of Blacks through hard work and education.

With groups that are roughly equivalent to the National Association for the Advancement of Colored People (NAACP), these future acronyms need to be remembered for …Chinese People (NAACP), Korean People (NAAKP), Lebanese People (NAALP), Ukrainian People (NAAUP) and let's not leave out the Brazilian People (NAABP). All of these groups, as well a hundreds more like them, will have advocates touting the need for financial aid for every ethnic group in the country. They will be successful because for universities to not give minority's preference would be blatant discrimination.

So keep saving for your child's college education. That child is going to need every cent you can save. College is expensive and will be increasingly difficult to get into if your child is an above average, involved, intelligent, well spoken and well-read American kid.

Other special rights that I think are just around the corner would further strain the relations between different groups of people. It won't be long before our nation will start to resemble a large-scale high school campus. Remember when the Jocks hung out here and the Geeks there? The Preppies gathered there and the Surfers over here. The Stoners met behind the school and the Chess club in the library. Well soon it'll be the ethnic clicks that will be picking on one another. Elitists will soon convince Chinese people that their ethnicity is more important than first being an American. Elitists will tell Muslims that their religion is more important than first being an American. In fact everything will soon be more important than first being an American.

"United we stand, divided we fall." "All for one and one for all." "You scratch my back, I'll scratch yours." There are many ways to say, " If we stick together we are a stronger entity than if we separate and stand alone or in small groups." Why do animals hunt in packs? Why do birds fly in flocks and fish swim in schools? Why should a nation stand together? Because there is more strength and protection, Period!

Elitists know this is true and they know that the only way to get us to break apart as a nation, is to put wedges between racial and ethnic groups, religious and special interest groups here in America. Fracture the foundation and the building will eventually crumble. Pit folks against each other long enough, and eventually there will be a real prejudice. Plant the seed of difference and a crop of resentment will grow. The Elites are masters of division and without a strong will, the people of America can look forward to a bumpy ride on the road to a nation divided.

If the Elitists get their way we will soon be so divided the United States will no longer exist. In the new utopia every conceivable group will have rights exclusive to that groups members, but no longer will these different groups live together. They'll just inhabit the same country.

# UTOPIA GOAL NUMBER 8
# ELIMINATION OF NATIONAL DEFENSE

Are you tired of living in the most powerful nation in the world? Do you think it is unfair to other nations that we are the only remaining superpower? Do you think we should destroy all of our weapons to prove to the world that we are striving for peace?

If you answered "Yes" to any of these questions then the new utopia will be the place for you! That's because Elites like to apologize for our country being so strong and for our willingness to use military power when we feel it's the right thing to do. Elitists want to rid our nation of weapons that make other countries feel threatened. Even terrorists would treat us better if we weren't always trying to stop them from killing people.

Peace through total lack of firepower seems like a very risky defense plan to me but ask any Liberal and they'll tell you it's the only way to go. That's because the liberal Elites think that if we pose no threat, that nobody will be offended or angered by us. If nobody is mad at us then we won't be attacked by anyone. That being the case, we will have no use for a defense system. Besides, weren't these weapons built to kill foreigners in the first place? How rude is that?

For all their self-proclaimed intelligence, the liberal Elites have a naive view of global events and international reality. In their bubble of peace and worldwide unity they are blind to the actual threats posed by nations who simply don't like us. Liberals can't stand the fact that we're not everybody's best friend and don't seem to understand that no matter what we do to appease foreign nations, we never will be. We cannot be friends with Israel without pissing off the Palestinians. Nor can we snuggle up to North Korea without upsetting damn near every democracy in the world. By throwing away our entire defense system to appease the French or Russia we leave ourselves wide open to attack from every single country around the globe. There are countless nations that would love to see us compromise our role as the world's superpower in the name of appeasement. In fact, disarmament would be the one thing America could do that would gain approval from Syria, Iran, North Korea and every other rogue nation in the world. To gain their approval (however brief it might be before they attack and destroy our nation) Liberals are willing to give up our national defense. Sacrificing national security for global approval is simply logical to Elite leaders. They are already embarrassed by the power we have and ashamed that we hold the title of "Superpower."

With a "Lead by example" attitude, it will simply be a matter of time before all other nations follow our example and destroy their countries defensive weapons. With crystal clear thought like this, it's a wonder that the elite leaders haven't convinced the rest of us yet, that this plan is the way to go.

Terrorists kill people by employing car bombs, hijacking airplanes, guns and poisonous gases. We kill terrorists for killing people by using missiles, tanks soldiers and guns. Wars between nations are fought with rockets, planes, battleships, submarines, missiles, bombs, tanks, soldiers, grenades and guns. There seems to be so much fighting between nations and between religious factions. According to elites, the reason is because there are so many weapons. Weapons become the medium of communications where once mediation and summits resolved conflicts.

By simply eliminating all weapons around the world we will in turn eliminate all conflict. Like the new utopia, all nations will presumably voluntarily destroy their nation's weapons and declare peace at last. Trillions of dollars will therefore be saved, as no future military spending would be necessary in the defense of our country.

After surrendering our arms and rolling into a ball like a defenseless amoeba, we can rest assured that we will be safe. There is no conceivable reason for any foreign nation or any group of people to attack our peaceful country, as we no longer pose a threat to anybody. Indeed there will be no way <u>for</u> them to attack us as soon as they follow our lead and dispose of their weapons.

When we can reason with madmen and rationalize with zealots, we can all come to an agreement to disarm. This could be as simple as negotiations over an espresso at a quaint cafe somewhere in France. Mr. Bin Laden and Senator Clinton can have an open conversation and learn to see eye to eye. Mr. Ill and Mr. Kerry could discuss a world without nukes and come to an agreement to disarm sometime before dinner.

Of course there will be bunkers and safe spots that will protect the new utopia's elite leaders in case this new defense strategy fails. These places will be well fortified with defensive weapons to insure the survival of liberal elites. The rest of the nation can afford to be sacrificed to test this new theory, but it probably won't come down to that. Wow, that makes me feel so much better.

We should count our blessing that Conservative leadership can objectively assess the threats posed to America by rouge nations around the world. We're lucky to be the world's "Damn superpower," even if it makes the Elites uncomfortable and ashamed. To stay free and to remain the most powerful nation in the world it is imperative to deny Liberals their chance to try out their "Peace through total lack of firepower" theory.

One of the many things Liberals fail to understand is that "If" this little social experiment doesn't work out the way they've envisioned, it will be the end of America, period! I know this is not necessarily a bad thing for self-hating Liberals, but for people like you and me, it might as well be the end of the world. Failure seems the only and obvious outcome to a utopian America without nukes. If you have them, you are not likely to need them. If you need them you'll be glad you have them.

"The best deterrent to war is a constant threat." It's a saying that's been around for years and I heard it first more than 25 years ago. That was my dad's answer to calm the worries I had after returning home one day after school. My grade-school teacher instructed the class that if we didn't destroy all of the world's nuclear weapons we would all die in the inevitable nuclear war to come. My dad explained the "Best deterrent" concept to me and to this day it makes sense.

## UTOPIA GOAL NUMBER 9
## CRIMINAL RIGHTS

This is a huge issue in the new utopia. It has been made apparent that in today's world criminals, serving prison time, are having their rights violated on a daily basis. There's no excuse for the treatment they receive in our penitentiaries and prisons while paying their debt to society.

Through news stories I have been made aware of the personal hardships these violent criminals endure while serving prison sentences for crimes like burglary armed robbery, rape, assault, kidnapping, child molesting, carjacking and murder. The rights of their victims were violated when they committed the crime and the rights of their families were violated when they hurt a loved one. But that doesn't seem to matter. What matters is that when the criminal was taken into custody the handcuffs were put on too tight and made the criminal's wrists feel uncomfortable. When taken to the police station to be questioned he was offered nothing to eat even though he was hungry. When booked on criminal charges he can't remember if the arresting officers read him his rights. When taken to jail he was forced to wear clothing that demeaned his dignity.

This is where the criminal rights activists really get going. They want to make the liberal elites aware of the violations perpetrated on these poor misunderstood souls while they're going through the legal system. We are to believe that a person should be shown pity, compassion and leniency if he has committed violent crime because the act itself was simply a cry for help. These criminal rights activists go as far to blame the victim for being in the wrong place or wearing the wrong clothes, thus forcing the criminal to perpetrate the act for which he is accused. "Suzan should not have been waiting for a bus that night. If she'd been somewhere else, my client would not have forced her into his car and raped her."

After being convicted of numerous charges and sentenced to a ridiculously short prison term, with eligibility for parole after half the term is served, criminals hire attorneys to sue over their treatment. It is true that there are times when a criminal might feel constrained while incarcerated. He may be denied certain privileges like sports or television at certain times while behind bars. They might not be served the food that they are accustomed to eating. And yes, there is a chance that he may be beaten up by other prisoners. Why these issues have been brought up and why they are now given any consideration is a mystery to me.

It seems to me that if a prisoner has a poor experience while being punished for criminal behavior, he might just be deterred from committing criminal acts in the future. It's a bit like getting grounded as a child. If a child on restriction could have friends over, go out and play, watch TV, play video games and enjoy dessert after dinner, then what would deter them from again perpetrating the same act that got them that "punishment?"

Today's criminals already have it made on the inside. Thanks to prisoner advocates our violent criminals live quite well as compared to some citizens struggling to get by honestly in society. The old, "Three hots and a cot" rhetoric of the old days has given way to ridiculous privileges granted to rapists and murderers. In the state of Oregon, one county has approved travel-sized personal flat screen TV's in inmate's cells. In this case an inmate can earn enough money working inside or gather enough money from friends and family, to purchase his very own personal television set. Along with personal TV's, inmates are allowed to enjoy sports, music, tobacco products, family visits, time off for good behavior and free clothing.

To a struggling minimum wage earner, inmates seem to have it pretty well. To the families of violent crime victims, inmates are living a life of privilege and enjoying freedoms that their deceased relative can never again enjoy.

Why are convicted criminals pitied, protected and provided for? Why do prison inmates enjoy any privileges while serving their time? It's because elites and liberal activists feel that these criminals are already being treated too harshly for what they refer to as, their mistakes. Yes their misjudgments should be forgiven and yes they should be given second and third chances. Three strikes and your out has become three strikes and you "Walk." They "Walk" away from any serious jail sentence and any real consequences for violent criminal behavior.

Drug dealers are forever getting off the hook by squealing on bigger drug dealers who in turn walk free for providing the name of a drug importer. These deals don't punish equally from the bottom up. Instead, they let everybody but the head honcho go. Even though everyone up the ladder has broken the law and ruined lives as a result of selling the illegal drugs.

Drunk drivers are put back on the road after little more than a slap on the wrist and made to pay a nominal fine. After two or three offenses, and one or more drunk driving accidents, we are asked to consider the reason why this individual drinks. It's left to us to figure out what has made this person dependent on alcohol and it's our obligation to feel sorry for this poor soul. To defend his criminal actions the defense will tell sad stories of divorce or loss and demand compassion from those who judge the drunk's fate. Instead of being punished to the fullest extent of the law, the drunk driver might be forced to attend a diversion class or see a psychiatrist for 6 weeks.

When a criminal commits a rape it should automatically be determined that it wasn't his fault. First of all, the woman was asking for it. She was wearing clothing that actually made the rapist act the way he did. The defense will argue that his client was sexually mistreated as a child and that this should mitigate his actions. In the new utopia maybe we'll be convinced that not only should he be acquitted of his crime, he should also receive an apology from his victim for making him act in such a way. Sounds like the compassionate thing to do to me.

Murderers should never be held accountable for their actions either. Obviously if a person is capable of murder that person is insane. And as we're all too well aware, no insane person can be held responsible for his actions. Therefore, all murderers are automatically off the hook. Not that they don't need psychiatric attention. They should receive help as long as the offer of mental help doesn't offend them. This murderous individual has most likely come from a broken home and was possibly abused as a child. This is reason enough for mandatory sympathy on the part of any judge and jury. Compassion for the killers and apathy for the victims make the justice system a better place for criminals to be "Punished."

To further ease the pain and shame felt by criminals in the utopia to come, the sentencing laws would be greatly reduced.

> -Starting at the top, first-degree murder will be done away with as part of the insanity reasoning mentioned above. This will also apply to second-degree murder.

-Manslaughter, armed robbery and rape will be punishable by a one-year prison sentence with eligibility for parole after three months served.

-Lesser crimes like assault, burglary and auto-theft, will be punishable by a suspended sentence, a letter of apology to the victim and ten hours of community service.

This would reduce over-crowding in our prisons, eliminate the cost of approximately $70,000 per year to imprison a criminal and allow for a compassionate court system to give these misunderstood individuals a second (or third) chance.

The sooner criminals can feel better about themselves; the sooner they'll stop committing these silly crimes in order to get attention. Remember what the child psychologists who helped raise these criminals say, "Bad attention is better than no attention at all." And with that in mind, all criminal behavior can be both explained and eradicated at the same time.

# UTOPIA GOAL NUMBER 10
## ELIMINATION OF PROFILING

Airports, inner city police precincts, medical research labs, retail stores, gas stations, convenience stores. These and a thousand other places are where profiling takes place every day. The practice of profiling is a half step above racial discrimination and bigotry. Is there nowhere in an airport a Muslim with an AK-47 can go without being profiled? We still take notice of a Black youth in the inner city running down the street carrying a TV. And yes, clerks at a convenience store take notice of groups of teenagers wearing baggy clothes and carrying backpacks through the isles of candy and beer.

Why is it that unrefined people still use profiling to seek out criminals and identify danger? For example, it's a well known fact that ninety-eight percent of serial killers are White males between the ages of twenty-five and forty who've had a history of animal abuse in their past. To Liberals, it's unthinkable that police might focus on White males between the age of twenty-five and forty, who have had a history of abusing animals. *This* is profiling. It's the most insensitive and discriminating practice still in use today. In fact it offends progressive thinking Elites almost as much as common sense offends them. To make things right, if not totally inconvenient, the new utopia will require detectives in serial killing investigations to question one Hispanic, one Asian and one African-American for every White male they question. This will not help police solve the crime any faster and will in fact slow the process down, but it will be the politically correct thing to do.

We all know that terrorists who have committed atrocities around the world are eighteen to forty-five years old and of Middle Eastern descent. It is relatively easy to identify age and ethnicity; therefore we are able to pay a little extra attention to Middle Eastern men between eighteen and forty-five. They may be in an off-limits area of an airport, taking pictures of landmarks or bridges, paying cash for flying lessons, or attempting to buy a thousand pounds of fertilizer. All of these actions should trigger an alert to trained security and law enforcement personnel. But in the perfect world we'll give the Middle Eastern man the benefit of the doubt and question the eighty year old woman in the wheel chair waiting to board a plane, instead. This is the politically correct thing to do and it eliminates profiling of Middle Eastern men.

Liberals find the use of profiling so offensive that they'd rather put the safety of the nation's citizens at risk than use common sense to stop a criminal act. It's for this reason criminals can continue to commit crimes that could have been solved if only police where allowed to perform their jobs. The liberal's flawed thinking allows them to tell us that we should look at a six year old girl carrying a doll with the same scrutiny we look at a thirty year old Iranian man wearing a trench coat. It's polite and politically correct to see all people as the same, after all, we're all humans.

I'm sorry, but Ted Bundy and Richard Ramirez are not the same as my neighbor or my uncle. Hitler and Gandhi have more than one identifiable difference. The similarities between Fidel Castro and Tony Blair end with them both being leaders of their respective countries. This may sound cruel and insensitive, but it's true. This is yet another reason why I'll have such a hard time fitting into the new utopia.

Modern medicine just developed a drug that helps Blacks with an inherent race-specific problem with heart failure. Blacks are two and a half times more likely to suffer from heart failure than non-Blacks and heart failure claims 50% of it's victims within five years. Without racial and genetic profiling, it would have taken unknown additional years of research and testing to discover a medicine that can save thousands of lives. Should we have sacrificed the lives of thousands of Americans by not researching and developing this drug as quickly as we did? Would it have been more politically correct to ignore that fact that different races have different health problems that afflict them to a more or lesser extent than another race? Yea, yea, yea, I know. We're all the "Human Race."

After the tragedy of September 11, 2001, we knew the nationality, if not the names of the terrorists who flew airplanes into our buildings. Would it have been a good thing to question groups of South Americans and Lithuanian people so that Middle Easterners didn't get offended because we singled them out? If tomorrow America awoke to news stories of passenger planes being flown into more buildings, who would we suspect did it? If you're a Liberal you might think it was the Japanese or the Canadians. After all, they're just as likely to have committed these acts of terror as any Middle Eastern group. Remember, profiling offends the elites almost as much a *common sense* does.

Should there be a reason why I'd hesitate to go into a bank if I saw two men wearing ski masks and trench coats waiting outside the front door? Not in the perfect world. These are just two guys who are cold and a bit self-conscious of their bodies and therefore wear loose fitting coats.

How about walking in on a situation where a man in front of the counter is showing his new gun to a cashier behind the counter at your local convenience store? Innocent enough isn't it? It is if we make no assumptions that might offend somebody.

We've all seen television shows or watched an episode of American Justice that has feature a criminal profiler. It's intriguing to watch this specialized professional break down every aspect of the criminal. They can very accurately specify the age, race, gender, mental condition, area of residence, family history and even approximate height and weight of a wanted criminal. The fact that their profile of a killer or rapist narrows the focus of the investigation saves time and ultimately lives. It eliminates suspects that would otherwise require precious time and effort from investigators.

This is a fantastic advantage to law enforcement, but well-intended do-gooders on the Left, frown upon it. How could anybody who claims to care about the safety of America's population have the audacity to criticize a practice that keeps it safe? Liberals would rather endanger you and I, than offend a violent criminal by using profiling in his apprehension. Since this seems to be the case, I'm not so sure I need any compassion from our not-so-bright friends on the Left.

By demonizing the use of profiling and outlawing it's practice, the Elites are forcing us to ignore our innate sense of self-preservation. If we are forced to drop our guard and dismiss all of the sensory input we gather pertaining to a certain situation, or a certain group of individuals acting a certain way, we are walking targets for disaster.

To take the ridiculous request to eliminate profiling to the extreme, let's try a ridiculous scenario. If you boarded an American Airlines 747 flight to travel to your desired destination and you noticed the wing was bent and one of the engines was smoking, would you refuse to fly on the plane? Of course you would. You would exit the plane and tell folks that your flight on an A.A. 747 could have killed you had you not noticed it's mechanical and structural shortcomings. If this event changed your opinion on the safety of flying and you decided to never fly again, you wouldn't be alone. But in the Utopians perfect worldl, if you said that you'd never fly on an American Airlines 747 again, you'd be accused of profiling. Simply by deciding that particular plane, flown by that particular airline wasn't safe, you could be thrown into the evil and despicable class of "Profiler." Was it a privately owned Cessna single engine plane that nearly caused you your life? Was it a Horizon Airlines 707 that looked like it was about to fall apart? No, it was a particular model owned by a particular company. What really happened? You looked at a certain situation, considered the circumstances, weighed the outcome, and made an intelligent decision. This decision probably saved your life. In the quest for political correctness, we would have been asked to ignore the bent wing and smoking engine, remained on the plane and assumed all would be well. Where's the correlation between the airplane and the profiling of people? By singling out a certain type of person, with certain characteristics and displaying certain behavior, danger or even a tragedy may be avoided. I call it observation and deductive reasoning and common sense. The Elites call it profiling.

Speaking of ridiculous, lets try some scenarios on for size.

Scenario 1. A Montana cattle rancher notices a large number of his herd missing during a vaccination session. He's heard that other ranchers have had cattle gone missing and that a cattle rustler is to blame. The local sheriff is called in to investigate the allegations and he confirms a cattle rustler is stealing the rancher's cows. The sheriff should:

A. Look into a connection with Chinese mafia in the Chinatown area of San Francisco.

B. Contact the FBI and ask for cooperation setting up a roadblock for all Lithuanian-born travelers in the state.

C. Focus the investigation on a local resident with knowledge of cattle, suspicious behavior and possibly a criminal record.

Scenario 2. A convenience store in Watts is robbed at gunpoint. A witness saw a Black male about six feet tall, weighing around 180 pounds, shoot the clerk and leave with cash from the register. The LAPD should:

A. Question all Korean patrons of the store to obtain alibis from them.

B. Round up all money-laundering ex-convicts with bank accounts in the Caiman Islands.

C. Focus the investigation on local Black males fitting the description of the eyewitness.

Scenario 3. A passenger airplane traveling from Israel to Boston is hijacked. Demands to free Mohamed Albini and Jaffar Ali are made. If not freed from an American prison by the time the plane reaches Boston, it will be crashed. Authorities should immediately:

A. Check the flight list. Obtain the names of all senior citizens on the flight list and contact their families to find out if they held a grudge against the airline.

B. Ignore the threat as a silly joke being played on the control tower by a couple of mischievous pilots.

C. Search the flight list for members of a radical Middle-Eastern group who has two of its leaders in a US prison.

Scenario 4. A serial rapist is loose on a university campus. The campus and local police should focus their investigation on:

A. The janitor found with ropes, duct tape and a prescription for Viagra in his locker.
B. All serial rapists currently incarcerated.
C. Any male with ties to both the college and to the victims.

As tricky as these questions are, you and I can get most of these scenarios pegged with the use of a little common sense. Liberals, on the other hand, find each answer for each scenario to be as likely as the next. It makes them feel good that they are not succumbing to profiling. They can clearly display their intellectual superiority by rising above the urge to point fingers. You and I, using common sense and setting aside political correctness, are the reason profiling needs to be eliminated.

In the new utopia you'll need to remember to check all the skills that have kept you aware of your surroundings and alive, at the door. This includes profiling, assumptions, preconceived notions, judgments and common sense. This is the only way we can truly reach a more advanced, progressive and eventually perfect world.

# UTOPIA GOAL NUMBER 11
## CELEBRITY IDOLISM

The new utopia will be a haven for all who act, sing, or tell jokes for a living. Because they haven't been respected or idolized to the extent that they've deserved in the past, they'll be hoisted up on the new utopia's shoulders.

Intellectual giants such as Pauly Shore, Adam Sandler, Drew Barrymore and Jennifer Aniston; Leonardo DeCaprio, Bruce Springsteen and Jon Bon Jovi all need to have their political beliefs heard and respected. In fact, it would serve you well to adopt their beliefs because they're great entertainers and therefore intellectually superior to you and I.

By turning on one of the big three national news broadcasts, one can hear from any number of their favorite Celebrities that are either standing up for the downtrodden in a third world country, protecting trees in the mountains of Washington, or endorsing a fringe-left political candidate.

There appears to be endless number of causes that the Celebrities support and make contributions to. There are so many ribbons in Hollywood that the sheer number, size and color of the things are overwhelming. Ribbons that represent the preservation of the rain forest, for the fight against AIDS, to remind women of breast exams and a hundred others. These ribbons represent the true commitment of these Celebes (whenever their commitment is convenient for them.)

These causes benefit from the recognition of the celebrity spokesman who represents them. Everybody recognizes Sally Struthers as the mouth for starving kids in Africa. Elton John is the world's spokesman for the fight against AIDS. The list goes on and on. What happens for the cause is great; what happens to the celebrity is expected. Already so full of themselves for being the star of this movie or the singer of that song, their heads get even bigger. They actually think they're the reason the cause they endorse is being addressed. They feel superior to all of us who can't act, can't sing and certainly can't solve any of the world's problems like they can. This arrogance transcends to an air of superiority and a condescending attitude to anyone with an address outside of Hollywood or New York City.

With a few exceptions, their behavior is horrible and they find themselves in trouble with the law or their fans more often than not. It makes sense that with their poor behavior and their air of superiority that celebrities almost always come down on the side of the left. Some are relatively moderate Democrats, but most are far left extremists who have no problem with vocalizing the controversial diarrhea that spills from their mouths, while addressing a range of social and environmental issues.

The problems with these glamour junkies, is that adolescents and teens worship and adore them. Therefore, whatever spews forth from Puff Daddy's mouth is the absolute irrefutable truth to a sixteen-year old fan. If Matt Leblanc tells a reporter that George Bush is stupid, it becomes a fact among every teen that has ever watched Friends. It's never repeated that *Matt Leblanc* thinks the president is stupid, just that the president *is* stupid. When Sean Penn tells the camera that the war in Iraq is an illegal war and that we should pull our soldiers out as soon as possible, that's what you hear echoed by the politically naive youngsters in our country. As we all know, if you tell a lie often enough it will eventually become the truth.

The pompous Hollywood elites know for a fact that their opinions are highly respected by the little people in America. It has to be that way because their opinions are so much more valuable that the opinions of a grocery bagger, a janitor, or an accountant. Though they themselves usually come from humble beginnings, they soon fall into the ocean of hype and ego associated with the business. I recently learned that prior to being "Discovered," Brad Pitt used to be a bus boy and also chauffeured strippers to their dancing appointments to earn extra cash while trying to "Break into" acting. Now that he makes $20 million per picture, he thinks he's intellectually superior to the common American. Does money insure infallible thought? Does a truckload of cash mean a person's whacko ideas should be given merit?

Who is Barbara Streisand to tell me how to vote? She tells us that president Bush is a screw-up and too stupid to be in position of such power. She also tells us that if we want real change we should vote for John Kerry (or the next liberal front-runner), who will make everything better. Personally, I don't want change. Things are going along pretty well if you ask me. And the way a liberal president would make things "Better", frightens me. Does this make me an uneducated simpleton? If so, I'd much rather stick to my convictions than change my beliefs to catch the coat tails of the latest political trend.

Celebrities want to impose their values on the common folks in America. In their little bubble, they think the whole world is just like Hollywood. It might actually surprise some of the bubble people that the rest of America's citizens actually cook their own meals, drive themselves to their destinations and have never flown first class. In fact, some of us simpletons buy ninety-nine cent shampoo, drink domestic beer and stay married to the same person for decades. As shocking and appalling as this must be to the Hollywood elite, this is the way that the majority of America lives. Still, I'd be willing to bet that they think I'm exaggerating. I mean come on…who buys ninety-nine cent shampoo?

These entertainers are so out of touch with mainstream America, it's pathetic. But in their bubble they believe they *are* mainstream America and the rest of us are just fans who watch their movies or buy their albums. Everything they do is better. Everything they buy is better. The way they think is better. Their political beliefs and agenda's are better. Are these people you want to support? I certainly don't want to feed their ego any more than I already have.

I personally like to hear from today's rap stars when objective media interviews them. With such vile language and stories of violence and rape, the murder of their mother or a drive-by shooting, they have no respect for decency. When confronted with questions about the influence their music has on the children that listen to it, they reply with lame answers like "It's just a song, don't take it so seriously." They say that it's just the way they express themselves and that they are doing these songs <u>for</u> the kids. If one of these rap "Stars" throws some money to a charity that benefits children, they can wipe their conscience clean and say they support positive influences on children. Visit a sick child in the hospital and you've earned the right to sing about as many "Bitches" and "Ho's" as you want. You can glorify the murder of a member of another gang, but first you must do a Public Service Announcement asking children not to smoke cigarettes. The contradictions between their songs and their answers in interviews are obvious, but should not surprise you. After all, the Hollywood elites live in the "Do it if it feels good" world where consequences are somebody else's problem.

The recent actions and behavior of numerous actors and singers have limited my choices in entertainment. No longer do I listen to the music of Bon Jovi, formerly one of my favorite bands. Movies starring Sean Penn or Susan Sarandon, Tim Robbins and Kevin Costner are off my list of must-see features. Never again will I spend a dime on music by Springsteen or Madonna. I refuse to support individuals who have openly denounced our president's actions as illegal. They speak out about atrocities committed by our troops and how we've violated the rights of the terrorists that attacked us. They condemn the United States while showing compassion for enemy fighters. Some Hollywood types have actually come out and said they hope we lose the war on terror and that we deserve to get our butts kicked. These are certainly not people I'm going to hand $17.99 to, in order to buy their C.D. It seems to me that the talent possessed by these Hollywood elites is over shadowed by their incredible dimwittedness. I believe their actions boarder on treason and if I recall, that used to be a punishable offense.

More frequently, Elites are hoisting on their shoulders the extreme propagandists that spew forth hate and spite towards conservative America. The most notable is the recent liberal hoopla surrounding Michael Moore. More specifically, the left rallied around the "Documentary" Fahrenheit 9/11. The movie is supposedly based on fact, portrays President Bush as an evil conspirator who cuts deals without discretion in order to line the pockets of his family and friends. The Left used clips from the one-sided Bush-bashing "Documentary" in campaign ads for presidential candidate John Kerry. They used their friends in the "Main stream" media to repeatedly air clips and short segments of the movie, which portrays the Bush administration as corrupt and morally bankrupt. Interviews with Moore whipped the Left into a virtual frenzy that enjoyed nothing more than watching one of their own finally gain a little notoriety. It was irrelevant to Liberals that the man who made the movie rubs the majority of Americans the wrong way. It was also irrelevant that the content of the movie was a series of out of context quotes and cut and paste editing to portray the Bush administration as evil buffoons.

As we know, facts can't be allowed to get in the way of Bush-bashing. If the Left allowed little technicalities like that stand in their way, they'd never gain any ground. With Moore as their new hero and their heralded "Voice of truth", the Left charged full steam ahead into the presidential campaign. Their campaign leaders and the liberal media touted Moore as some sort of intelligent individual with a grasp on reality. Because Moore made outrageous allegations and "Showed" the corruption of the President and his administration, the Left avoided making those allegations themselves. Now they didn't have to gamble with the possibility that such accusations coming directly from the Left, would be looked upon as simply a typical political attack. With their butts off the hook, they threw their full support to the man who did their dirty work for them. With his new celebrity status, Michael Moore was booked for speeches at colleges and Universities across the country. During his fifteen minutes of fame, Moore spewed hate and disseminated half-truths and lies to thousands of America's college students. As Hollywood types touted his candor and rewarded his "Courage" to stand up to the big bad Right, they joined together to form a united Hollywood front against Bush and his leadership. In Hollywood, patriotism is equated with dissention and conservatism is equated with evil. Self-hate is somehow revered as noble, and national pride is simply not tolerated. Are these the individuals you want to reward with your hard earned dollar? Let's show a little restraint and stop supporting these "Actors" whose most difficult role is attempting to sound intelligent.

Another propagandist that the Left silently loves is our favorite professor from Colorado, Ward Churchill. The only reason the Left hasn't come out and publicly backed the comments of Mr. Churchill is because he seems to be a little rough in his comparisons of 9-11 victims to Nazis. Mr. Churchill has no problem voicing his opinion that those who died in the World Trade Center deserved their fate due to their belief and participation in capitalism. He said that what happened to our fellow citizens was the next logical step in the punishment of those who believe in the ideals of America. This isn't to say that Elites don't believe everything he says is true, but like Michael Moore; they have to let him test the waters of public opinion before voicing their congratulations and support. Committing to Ward Churchill's point of view too soon would reveal a little too much about the true beliefs of liberal Elites. They must tread carefully so as to not tip their hand.

So, before echoing the sentiments of former gas station attendants and bus boys, who now make more in a week than you and I will make in a lifetime, think about what they're saying. Just because they can act doesn't mean their political ideas hold any water. They may be able to carry a tune, but their opinions carry no weight. We have to educate our star-struck youngsters about the beliefs these Elites hold for our country. If kids really knew how these people felt about America, maybe they wouldn't hold them in such high regard.

# UTOPIA GOAL NUMBER 12
## OBJECTIVE MEDIA

Remember that your idea of objective and Hitler's idea of objective may differ a little. In the new utopia objective media will mean reporting a story that sheds the best light on liberal causes while completely ignoring the conservative ones. Not that Dan Rather or Tom Brokaw haven't already figured out how to do this, it's just not a network mandate yet.

To watch the news on ABC, NBC, CBS and CNN, one would get the impression that the war in Iraq is an illegal war because Mr. Bush didn't get approval from the U.N.. You might get the impression that removing Sadam from power only worsened the living conditions of Iraqis. And certainly we should all be aware that the war in Iraq is a quagmire and another Vietnam. Their reports describe how the US troops morale is extremely low, there are insufficient numbers of troops to win the war and at this rate, there will be another military draft under the leadership of George Bush.

They are the conduits of bad news. The "Big three" hate the current administration, their reports and reporters constantly look for stories that shed a negative light on anything the President does. This affects the way the country views all events in today's world. In the land of pessimism, mainstream media digs to find the worst of every issue. The war had been a great example of one-sided reporting and shows that the media truly has an agenda. How many stories about the abuses of prisoners at Abu Graib made the front page of newspapers or kicked off the nightly news broadcast? The media pounded the story of US soldiers intimidating terrorist suspects and treating them poorly. Countless pictures and videos were shown and analyzed over and over again. The continuous and ongoing reports that lasted for months on end would have you believe that the US Armed Forces were all corrupt and ruthless criminals. One-sided reporting showed prisoners wearing a dog leash, stripped of clothing, being forced into close proximity of a dog, or humiliated with sexually suggestive poses. Wow! We hurt the feelings of enemy prisoners. Appalling isn't it? Humiliating these poor souls…. While their brothers in arms are cutting the heads off Americans and our allies. Yea, how long did stories run about the beheading of Nicholas Burg or any of the others that died at the hands of Muslim extremists? A day or two at most. And wasn't the video of the beheading horrendous? Oh, that's right, nobody showed the video of the atrocity. Why? Because the media didn't think it was appropriate and that Americans didn't need to see what real brutal behavior looks like. They'd hate to inspire outrage against our enemy.

Extending the coverage of the beheadings and executions might rally support for our goal to fight these animals in Iraq. If that happens, then support for an unwavering President Bush would grow as well. The media hates Mr. Bush. Therefore, these stories must be touched on, and then forgotten before damage to the left's agenda can be done.

Apparently the news elites think the common American is too stupid to take unbiased facts presented to them in a professional fashion, interpret them and form an opinion. Therefore, the news media must do it for us. Unfortunately the "Facts" they report have already been put through the liberal agenda processor and by the time they get to our television sets, the stories are slanted and pre-digested for us. These preconceived thoughts leave little room for personal opinions to be formed.

This is exactly how the elites want it to be. They tell us their version of a story and then inform us how it should be perceived. The mainstream media has been pulling this trick on the American people for decades. It wasn't until FOX came along that we found there was also good in all of the stories that were being reported. The reporting of positive things is damaging to the elite's agenda at a time in history when Republicans are in power. Likewise, when the democrats were in power, all we heard from the mainstream media was how fantastic everything was. Little things like scandals and criminal acts were poo-pooed and anything that looked a bit shady was averted and excused. When questions were raised by FOX news about these shady acts, Americans were finally able to get a glimpse of the truth without the filter that the media had been providing for its heroes on the left.

We are bombarded not only by the bad things happening during wartime, but how bad things are at home with the environment, with health care and with social programs. To listen to the media elites, there hasn't been a good thing accomplished domestically since the Republicans gained control of the House and Senate. The new prescription plan is just a pacifier to keep the senior citizen's votes rolling in. Due to lax environmental policy our nation is on the verge of an environmental catastrophe. You hear stories every day about the starving and downtrodden right here in America as a result of spending cuts to social programs. If things were really as bad as reported by the media, wouldn't this country be in a monumental uprising, the like of which hasn't been seen in over two hundred years? I'd think the nation would be in shambles and visions of a post apocalyptic society would come to mind.

Another blatant example of media bias is the total lack of investigative reporting concerning the U.N.'s oil for food scandal. Fox news covered the events unraveling at the U.N. on a daily basis. The "Mainstream" news has yet to acknowledge that a scandal exists or that the U.N. is guilty of skimming billions of dollars from the program. Instead they cover puff pieces about the most recent celebrity trial or who won what Oscar for which America-bashing movie. They insult our intelligence every single day and without other news coverage from more objective sources, we wouldn't even realize it. We perceive the truth to be what we can see and hear. When all the majors tell us the same things and omit topics they should be reporting on, how are we to know what is really taking place in the world? By not reporting on major events such as the U.N.'s oil for food scandal, the media is dangerously close to conducting a cover-up.

In many cases the "Mainstream" media distorts, if not outright fabricates what it is reporting. Phony documents, unfounded allegations and careless reporting have been topics in the public's eye for some time now. Poor research and falsehoods have ruined some individuals and smeared the reputation of others. Seldom is the case when the "Mainstream" media turns on itself and cannibalizes one of it's own. This is why reports and reporters defend liberal figureheads and promote stories that shed positive light on Elites and their agenda. Similarly, the same media try's to smear Conservatives by magnifying anything that sheds a negative light on the Right. It's mountains out of molehills if it sheds a negative light on Conservatives. Touch-and-go reporting, if not total omission of misdoings for Liberals. We are to believe this is fair and objective reporting. As I stated earlier, it becomes the truth if you hear it from a tie wearing, slick-looking anchorman on the *American Broadcasting Company*, right?

More Americans are getting their news from alternate sources than ever before. This fact has allowed millions of us to open our eyes to the actual truths in the world. This is good for those individuals who have relied on the judgment of liberal biased news producers in the past. To the chagrin of "Mainstream" media, their viewing public has drastically declined in numbers. We know competition in the marketplace generates lower prices and better deals. Maybe some long overdue competition in the media will generate honest and competent reporting from our former favorite newscasters. A focus on more of the positive and less time spent magnifying the negative would be a great starting point for the gloom and doom networks. It's just a suggestion.

Thank goodness things are actually going well in our country. The poor are looked after. The environment is healthy and the war on terror is being won. I hate to sound optimistic but the fact is, I don't hate our President and can actually muster a nice thing or two to say about the job he and his administration are doing. As unpopular as this may seem to our media elites, this simpleton has actually formed his own opinion and will stick with his beliefs. Not that my opinion will matter much in the new utopia. The news will be provided directly by the liberals in power and be reported as needed to keep liberals in a positive light.

# Utopia Goal Number 13
## Drug Legalization

If the banning of religion and the removal of morals aren't enough to break down the fabric of America, then the next logical step down our road of destruction is to legalize drugs. Isn't it the next logical step in destroying any values that still may remain in our society? If liberals can accomplish this goal, the end will be much closer than most of us realize.

The battle has been going on in individual states for years. The legalization argument surfaces under many different guises. In my state, the legalization of marijuana is disguised as the "Medical Marijuana" law. It's been touted as a bill of mercy and we've all been told that any *compassionate* person has to agree that the legalization of pot is necessary. The Liberals are trying to warm the water a little bit by first by attempting to legalize pot for medicinal purposes. Once that has been accepted, it will be much easier to legalize the drug for "Adult use only," and later it'll be determined that pot use is "Safe for all."

With any luck, the liberals will be able to make the use of pot as common as drinking a glass of wine. It doesn't matter that they've banned cigarette smoking just about everywhere but in your own private bathroom; Liberals will encourage the public use of the newly legal product.

Advertising campaigns will focus on getting the youngsters involved and lighting a joint. It may even be promoted as a family activity. I can see the billboard now:

Missing out on your kid's lives?
Wonder what they do while your at work?
Take the time to find out how they are! Fire up a joint
and sit down with the kids for a little "Family time."

Doesn't that sound like the perfect forum to discuss the importance of values with your children? "Go get the rolling papers Johnny, then sit down here and tell me what you're doing in English class."

I don't see why the legalization of drugs would need to end with marijuana when there are so many mind-destroying drugs available to assist Liberals with the destruction of our society. I could easily see the Liberals fighting for the legalization of cocaine for its numbing value. "It's vital for do-it-yourself home dentists to have cocaine available." Maybe LSD could be useful in stimulating imagination in children. "Little Johnny's imagination has really taken off since we started him on two doses a day." Methamphetamines would be another great drug to legalize due to its low production costs and could provide the do-it-yourself home dentists with plenty of patients.

Of course the real purpose of legalizing drugs is to further tear down the fabric of this country. The stated purpose for the legalization of these drugs is to tap into the tax opportunities of products that are currently being used, but not exploited. Think of the money that could be raised by assessing a twenty percent "Pot tax." Or a thirty percent "LSD Fee." There would be a plethora of social programs that could finally be funded if only we could legalize and tax drugs.

Does it make sense to raise funding for mental health programs by legalizing and taxing mind-altering drugs? If you're a Liberal this sounds like a logical and well thought out plan. There's nothing that calms a schizophrenic like a good hit of acid. A couple of puffs off a joint ought to relax the repetitious behavior of the person suffering from Obsessive-Compulsive Disorder. How about treating a client's depression with a line of cocaine? Brilliant!

Employers would be in a world of hurt. Already I've heard of a case in which a medical marijuana patient sued his employer for not allowing him to operate heavy equipment while he was stoned. Did you get that? The guy sued because he wasn't allowed to operate heavy equipment while he was *stoned*. What could possibly be next? Mandated pot-smoking breaks for employees? "Hawaiian hemp Fridays" at the office? Office Christmas(oops, Holiday) parties decorated with cocaine candy canes? A school smoking area that would cater to the needs of marijuana smokers? That would be a good one. Imagine classroom refrigerators stocked with pizza and couches set up in front of multiple T.V. sets, all tuned to cartoon network. Just what a school needs to teach our students.

Liberal leaders would really have an easy time instituting their agenda if they could keep citizens constantly stoned. We'd all be a bunch of dope-smoking, Twinkie-eating, couch potatoes that would offer little resistance to anything as long as we had a full bag of weed. Not a lot of angry stoned folks out there, are there? Everything seems to be O.K. When they want to raise our taxes we could smoke a joint and say "That's cool man." When they want to move us off our rural land we could smoke a joint and say "That's cool man." When they attempt to sterilize us because they don't think we need more than 1.7 children, we can smoke a joint and say "That's cool man." Yea, I can't imagine too many confrontational stoners. As long as we were in a good supply of dope the Left could do just about anything they wanted while facing minimal resistance.

If you think I sound just a little paranoid, think about this. It's hard to imagine why anyone would want to legalize the use of substances that have been proven to destroy our brain cells, cause death by overdose and ruin the lives of our families and children. Can you come up with any logical reason to make these harmful substances more readily available than they already are? The simple fact that liberals have fought to do just that ought to be enough reason for you to question their motives. We know drugs destroy, so why would we want to make them more prolific in society if we know the general public will suffer as a result? Kind of makes you wonder, doesn't it?

# UTOPIA GOAL NUMBER 14
## EXPANDING SOCIAL PROGRAMS

If you think that our social programs are out of control today, wait for the programs that will be instituted by the elites in the new utopia.

Before we discuss the reasons why social programs have spiraled out of control we must first establish the reason why social programs exist. Originally, the purpose of social programs was to assist a person who could not afford basic human needs such as food, shelter and medical attention. It also helped those in our society who could not help themselves due to situations beyond their control. Food stamps were once used by very poor families to purchase flour, sugar, rice, beans and other staple items that ensured they wouldn't starve to death. Medical fees have been based on a sliding scale so extremely low-income individuals can receive medical care virtually free of charge. Financial aide was given to families who would otherwise be forced to move out of their house, leaving them homeless.

These programs were started with the best of intentions to help our country's poorest citizens with basic needs until they could afford to support themselves. If those who used these social programs today had two things, the programs might still work. The two things that have been eliminated in today's program users are *pride* and *dignity*. They no longer look for temporary assistance, but for long-term caregivers.

The reason our social programs are so large and out of control, is because people have been conditioned to look for a hand-out wherever they can. Fifty years ago people were ashamed to have to ask for help feeding their family. They almost had to be forced by neighbors or fellow church members to accept assistance. They were also very grateful for the assistance they received because they knew it was not the responsibility of others to look after their family's well being. These folks had pride and dignity and couldn't get out of the jam that required them to accept assistance, fast enough. Having been in the position of requiring help themselves, they were also the first to offer assistance to others they knew were in need. This is how the private sector served to help those in need. Things have changed!

## Food Stamps

In today's world of big government, there are social programs for just about everything. The problem with the programs is that they count on the users to become reliant on the assistance they provide. Food stamps are no longer used to buy rice and beans to insure a family doesn't starve to death. Today, food stamps are used to purchase soda and ice cream so the kids don't feel like they're going without. Assistance that was given on a short-term basis until a family was back on its feet, has morphed into an ongoing assistance that has now continued for up to three generations.

The government has conditioned people to look for hand-out's by taking the stigma of receiving help, away. They told us "Don't let your pride get in the way." They told us, "We'll take care of you." They asked, "What other needs might we be able to assistance you with. Before long the government was paying half the bills for a quarter of the families in the country.

Americans used to be leery of "Get something for nothing" promises. Now we *expect* something for nothing. The price of free assistance is higher than anyone expected. Nothing is free and the price paid for the services provided by social programs is an individual's ongoing dependence on that service. Liberals have made living in poverty so comfortable that very few individuals are motivated to work their way out of it. Especially devoid of personal pride and personal ownership is the second and third generation of welfare recipients. These individuals are the result of a social experiment that helped people so much that eventually the people could no longer help themselves. Lazy and dependent on the system, these folk are just where Liberals want them. By supplying them with food, shelter and cash assistance every month, they control every facet of their lives.

They also have control of their votes when elections roll around. All that needs to be done to insure the "Poor" vote is for the Liberals to make promises that sound good to those dependent on assistance. "If you vote for me I'll fight for increases to your food stamps dollars" The more programs these folks are dependent on the more they'll benefit if their favorite Liberal is elected. I see this as the practice of Liberals buying votes, but it's been planned and developed so well that my view is in the minority. It has become accepted and expected that the nation's low-income individuals generally vote Democrat.

Now we have a brief overview of why assistance was originally offered and what it has evolved into thus far:

Now let's take a closer look at food stamps. Some of the "Needy" families that receive as much as $350 each month to buy their groceries, would be able to feed their families if they'd spend their own grocery dollars wisely. I know what feeding a family of five costs. I also know that I'd go broke trying to feed my family pizza, hot pockets and dozens of other prepared foods every night. The average large pizza is now over $20. It would take two pizzas to feed my family and as my boys grew, maybe three. Toss in a six-pack of soda and some ice cream for dessert and you could easily spend $70 for a single dinner. That equates to a weeks worth of groceries for my family, if I were to be responsible with my food budget. The question low-income folks are asking when this point is brought up is, "Why be responsible if you get free money for food every month?"

The list of items approved for purchase with federal food stamp dollars is staggering. A few of the most shocking things that can be purchased with "Free food dollars" are Lobster, T-bone steaks, prawns, boneless skinless chicken breasts, crab legs, soda, candy bars, ice cream, and premium coffee blends.

The list is far more extensive but the point is if you're eating at my table, you'll eat what I serve. This means that restrictions should be put on the items that food stamp recipients should be allowed to purchase. How many pounds of rice, beans, pasta, and tomato products could be purchased for the price of one lobster tail? Why does a family that "Relies on food stamps to put food on the table", need top dollar luxury items that most of the rest of Americans can only afford a time or two a year? The buying strategy of choice for many of the low-income food stamp recipients is to purchase all the groceries they need with food stamps and then use their cash for the beer and cigarettes that food stamps refuse to cover. "Refuse?" Why should the poor be refused <u>anything</u>?

Advocates for the poor tell us how cruel we are for suggesting that we limit the choices of low-income "Shoppers." Unable to convince congress to pick up the cost of their smoking and drinking habits, they still dutifully remind us that just because they're poor, they should not be limited in what food items they choose to feed their families. I think I need an advocate to remind car dealers that just because I can't afford a new Hummer, it's no reason why they shouldn't hand over the keys.

To politicians, the food stamp program keeps poor voters happy and in full support of those who will continue to fight for their shopping rights.

## Housing Assistance

This is another social program that needs to be seriously overhauled. Housing and Urban Development disburses millions of federal dollars ( read: your and my tax dollars) to cover the cost of housing for individuals and families throughout the country each year.

Now, I'm all for helping an individual who is in need and is willing to help himself, but I'm tired of throwing good money after bad to support those who choose to be complacent. What happened to the mind-set of "Necessity is the mother of invention," or "Struggle breeds strength?" Without requiring something of these folks they'll never persevere.

I drive by HUD approved housing and low-income HUD apartments daily on my way home from work. Here are folks who are sitting on their '"Paid for" apartment patios, smoking cigarettes and drinking beer with friends and/or neighbors. It is my opinion that if they can afford tobacco and alcohol products that they don't need my generosity to cover the expense of their housing costs. I'm already paying for the T-bone on their grill.

The low-income housing advocates have convinced congress that there is a huge need for subsidized housing. Then, the liberal decision makers, whose compassion is a mask for control and power, allocate millions to help these folks who have chosen not to help themselves.

There is a distinct difference between compassion and coddling. In the past America has been compassionate in regards to our fellow citizens. The private sector has always done what has been needed to see that friends and neighbors were taken care of. Over the past couple of decades compassion has evolved into coddling, and coddling has become big business. Big government business! With the ever-expanding social programs, including annual increases in the amount of dollars spent on housing, the government is less compassionate and more coddling than ever. They continue to lower the qualifications and requirements thus making more people eligible for assistance. Then they turn around after putting more people on assistance roles and tell congress they need more money because there's been an increase in participation.

The future utopia will be a place where food and housing costs will be eliminated for anybody who has just enough money to buy cigarettes and booze. There is no excuse for low-income people to be required to sacrifice their habits for food or shelter. This compassion will continue to create bigger government and further citizen's dependence on the system. A goal of the liberal left.

In our new advanced society, we can expect to see social programs that have been neglected thus far. These would be programs that the damn Republicans just wouldn't approve of in the past. Remember the "Add-a-dick-to-me" surgery that changed the sex of a female to a male? Liberals thought this should be covered by insurance and that the surgery was justifiable. They thought it would resolve some internal conflict the person receiving the procedure might be having. Republicans wouldn't go for it. Those damn folks just didn't understand the pressures put on trans-gender, trans-sexual members of our society. How callous and cold these folks could be.

New social programs will include the "Man-Womb Implant Program." This is an absolute must-have social program. It will be decided that it is unfair that only women have the chance to experience childbirth and that such a beautiful phenomenon should not be restricted to a certain sex. It would work as follows. Gay couples who wanted to have biological children together would petition for a MWIP hearing where it would be decided that the couple qualifies for the procedure. A surgical team would then install a womb into the "Wife" and start the fertilization process. In nine months "Ted" and "Lance" would be the proud parents of a new baby. Of course this would cost taxpayers plenty of money, but it's a program that is just as important as any in existence today. Actually, it would almost be inhuman not to offer this service to gay men with the desire to have children.

Another important social program will be the "Drug and Alcohol Dependant's Supply Program," or the DADSP. It's a known fact that drugs and alcohol can foster a chemical dependence for those who use them. It's also a fact that withdrawal symptoms for an addict attempting to quit using drugs, can be uncomfortable, and in certain cases quite severe.

It's due to the difficulty of quitting substance use that the leaders of the new utopia will denounce the importance of quitting the use of drugs and implement the DADSP. To pay for the continued use of drugs is cheaper than spending federal funds on programs to help people quit. And unlike treatment programs that can't guarantee an addict won't return to using drugs, the DADSP will have a 100% success rate of keeping the addicts addicted. Without a shortage of drugs amongst the druggies and a plentiful supply of booze for the drunks, much of societies criminal activity will be reduced. Ask any officer at your local police station or sheriff's department and they'll tell you that theft and burglary are often the crimes of choice that allow druggies to get their fix. How great is it that this social program will reduce crime and at the same time, reduce human suffering in cases were withdrawal would normally be the byproduct of quitting drugs? What's the lesson we all need to learn here? High druggies are happy druggies! And individual happiness is the responsibility of the government.

How about school student's rights in the new utopia? We've been demanding and expectant of these youngsters long enough! Good Grades based on correct answers and a rigid 8:00 am start-time has put undue stress on children in America for far too long. The new utopia will work with student rights activists to create the new "Student's Dignity Act." The SDA will be a guideline requiring teachers and administrators to treat students in such a way that the students are not put under pressure to perform or any stress related to curriculum or workload. Respect for student's verbal and stylistic expression will also be a top priority for students attending class in the new utopia. The social program that will police the school staff will be responsible for providing legal assistance to students who feel they've been subjected to treatment not prescribed in the SDA guidelines.

Citizen's tax dollars will pay the salaries of no less than two "Student Activist Observers" in each classroom in the country. An investigation in the issuance of any grade lower than a "C" will be required, until all grades issued are "above average." This way the American people can actually pay for the nation's children to be functionally illiterate and educationally challenged. Another social program to the rescue.

Lets talk about a social program that would provide "The American Dream," to all those unwilling to work towards this goal on their own. In the new utopia, the "Right to pursue happiness" will be modified and will read, "Guarantee of your personal happiness." This means that a whopper of a social program would be in charge of the happiness of any and all underachievers. Now this may sound like a big job, but after all, it's up to the government to supply the things needed to make it's citizens happy. Things like television sets will be provided to everyone who thinks a TV will make them happy. Additional TV's will be provided to unhappy people who have too few TV sets. A car is a must-have to obtain real happiness and a newer car is required for anyone driving an old one. If a one-story house is too small, then a two story will be built to replace it. There will be few, if any, happiness-inducing tangible objects that will not be covered by this program. It's so hard to believe that the citizens of America were once expected to pursue happiness on their own, isn't it?

I know these new social programs may seem a bit exaggerated and far-fetched but remember that these programs will be run by Elites who've already promised to eliminate the need for wheelchairs among paraplegics and to instill peace in the Middle East without the use of force. If they can accomplish these miracles why would they stop there? There would be plenty of money for the new program if we didn't have to spend money on war and weapons and if we raised your taxes just a bit more. If we can take from those who have and give to those who don't have, then we've reached true enlightenment. Ahhh capitalism, freedom and personal choice at it's best. To a liberal, "The social program" is the nation's greatest renewable natural resource.

# UTOPIA GOAL NUMBER 15
# THE ELIMINATION OF COMMON SENSE

Common sense has been the bane of the liberals for as long as there have been liberals. It's very difficult to promote ideas of the ridiculous and laws of the asinine when people use their common sense. Too many things have become tolerated, accepted and even expected due to the constant dulling of America's common sense. In fact, in many circumstances, it's often offensive to use common sense when forming opinions or making decisions when it comes to things of the weird.

In 1950, if you asked 100 people what would happen if you prohibited the logging industry from cutting trees, the response would go something like this. "Well, the loggers would be put out of work, the mills would shut down. The economy would suffer and the price of lumber would skyrocket." After 55 years, a lot of alternative thought and the dulling of common sense, we've actually convinced some Americans (even leaders in congress and some influential judges with no common sense) to ban loggers from logging. The consequences of this decision are the same as our 1950's counterparts had predicted. But here in the land of the weird, the decision is considered to be intelligent and well thought out. Isn't it outlandish to think we should use the natural resources put on this earth for human benefit?

Try this one on for size. Does common sense dictate that people who do bad things, be punished? Over the course of history, criminals have been fined, jailed, whipped, hanged and beheaded as punishment for crimes of varying degrees. Common sense tells us that a criminal who is punished will be deterred from committing that crime again. The worst-case offenders are removed from society in order to keep society safe. Here in the land of the weird, where common sense is cruel and insensitive, criminals receive disproportionately low punishment for the crimes they commit. This, because our progressive thinkers want to understand the criminal and justify his actions. Remove responsibility by removing common sense from the opinion-forming process and your left with today's criminal justice system. The very system that turns killers free and rewards rapists with weekend furloughs. Make sense to you?

Common sense tells us that a marriage is between a man and a woman. Ask anybody twenty years ago what marriage is and you'd hear "When a man and a woman take a sacred bond to commit to each other for life," or " When a woman and a man vow to love each other forever." Look at today's legal battles over gay marriage. Does it make sense that Americans should have to pass laws that should be recognized as simple common sense? No! But we're doing just that because common sense isn't so common anymore.

Does it make sense that a person who felt he was gaining weight, cut back on food and maybe mix a little exercise into his daily routine? Facts show that one can lose weight by taking in fewer calories than one is expending. Diet and exercise are the only proven way to safely lose weight. In today's "Liberalized" world things are looked at differently. Step 1: To lose weight in today's backwards world, one must first get fat by eating two or three times the recommended daily caloric intake at any number of fast-food places while being as physically stagnant as possible.

Step 2: Said overweight person then hires a lawyer and sues the nearest fast-food chain for his weight gain. Step 3: An activist judge who despises the profits being made by McDonald's or Burger King decides to punish them. He makes them pay a million dollars to the slob who got fat by eating too much of the food that he knew was bad for him in the first place. Now you have a fat, rich guy who can afford to eat out even more. Maybe restaurants should make every overweight person who walks through their doors sign a disclaimer before ordering. I forgot! That would be profiling.

Common sense tells us that children need to be raised, taught and influenced by their parents. It used to be mom and dad's responsibility to teach manners, courtesy, morals and even to punish a child if that child misbehaved. With common sense just a fuzzy memory, some of the parents in this generation have no idea what to do with the child once they've created one. The liberal elites tell us it's not our fault if we can't deal with our children. They've all but taken away the right for us to punish our children. They give children more rights than the parents who are trying to raise them. For example, in Washington a judge ruled in favor of a seventeen year old girl who sued her mother for eavesdropping on one of her phone conversations, citing invasion of privacy. The mother said it was the only way to find out what her "Out-of-control" child was doing. The incorrigible child won and the parent who told her, "It's my house, it's my phone, it's my rules and it's my right to know what you're doing," lost. Liberals also think that spending thirty or forty hours a week staring at a television set or playing video games is nothing more than a hobby the kids are "Involved with." Does destroying the lives of so many children by teaching them little and holding them accountable for nothing, make any sense to you?

Certainly it makes sense to expect the most from students in school, right? The higher the standards, the more the child has to work and thus, the more a child learns. This approach to education has worked in America. It produced a well-educated and well-rounded society. It wasn't until the Elites started lowering the standards so the learning curve was based on the comprehension skills of the poorest student in the class, that we started graduating functionally illiterate students. Education is a threat to the liberal Elite's agenda. They've found a way to make us think we're still sending our children to school to become educated, while at the same time making educational standards so low that little is learned by the nation's students. Common sense has become so blurry that many Americans don't realize this is happening.

How about the use of force in war? Capture or kill the enemy before they capture or kill you. Ring any bells? Sure, Americans have integrity and rules of engagement, but our goal is to win a war by incurring the fewest casualties necessary, while inflicting irreparable damage to our enemy. American soldiers have been trained in the use of force and the tactics that insure a victorious outcome. Elites, who enjoy nothing more than seeing America fall on its face, are hard at work to remove common sense from the battlefield. They want us to win the respect of our enemies by fighting "Sensitive battles." They condemn the treatment of enemy soldiers while defending the executions and assassinations of Americans. They report on every negative aspect of the war while failing to report on any accomplishments or positive outcomes achieved by our efforts. They criticize the use of force by our troops and demand court-martials for soldiers who kill enemies during battles. They second guess every tactic and strategy and tell us how ignorant we are when, in the course of war, something unexpected arises.

Common sense tells me to support our troops by giving them the support and materials they need to win the war and get back to their families. Liberals say they support the troops but oppose the war and then do all they can to undermine the actions of our military. They vote against the supplies and tools needed to insure safety and victory for our military. They deny our nation's soldiers the very things they criticize the President for not supplying the troops with. There are actually Americans in this country that are actively rooting for our enemy to win. This means they want nothing more than to see our military fail. Don't their actions speak for their intent? It's reasonable to assume that if the enemy is winning it's because they're inflicting more damage on our troops than we are inflicting on theirs. It would also go to figure then, that more American soldiers would be killed and injured. Yet, Liberals tell us that those who are wishing for our military to fail are offended when we call them unpatriotic. We're constantly reminded that they're just as patriotic as you and I.

Does it make sense to you that those who "Support" our troops by wishing for their deaths, be defended as patriots? A hundred years ago they'd have been called traitors, convicted of treason and strung up in the public square. In fact, the Liberals waited with great anticipation of the confirmation of the "One Thousand American Soldiers Killed In Iraq," story to hit the press. The Elites look at the ultimate sacrifices paid by our military men and women to keep America safe and free, as nothing more than political fodder. They use it for the sole purpose of criticizing the President and his administration. How much of this shameful treacherous and obscene behaviors are we willing to tolerate before peoples blood starts to boil? When will Liberals actually find themselves in physical danger from a society who recognizes treason when it sees it? And don't give us that "We're just as patriotic as you are" crap! Common sense blurred again.

Here's another brain bender courtesy of the wacky Left. The principal and school board of a high school in Cupertino California, has determined that the teaching of the constitution to its students is *unconstitutional.* I actually had to listen to the story a couple of times to be sure that what they were saying was what I had heard. Yep! The teaching of the constitution, one of the most important documents in the history of mankind, is not allowed in one of *America's* high schools because it references God. In the very same town of Cupertino, it is required for 7th grade students to wear clothes worn by traditional Muslims and to complete five Muslim prayers in order to graduate to eighth grade. A reference to God is a bit different than promoting Christianity by forcing students to read the bible and recite scripture in order to pass a class. At the same time they're requiring American children to dress like Osama Bin Laden and pray to Allah if they wish to be promoted to the next grade level. This is the epitome of hypocritical and asinine and proves that common sense is not in the vocabulary of the Liberals! I knew it wouldn't be long before this new attack on common sense would spread like a bad rash. Read on!

Three days after hearing the shocking story of elitists banning the Constitution from being taught in the classroom, the Libby's eliminated the use of the Declaration of Independence as a teaching aid due to it's controversial content. If I'm not mistaken, these are the very documents that ensure their rights....to ignore these documents? How many clichés about biting noses to spite faces, stepping on toes, looking a gift horse in the mouth, could we all come up with to describe the stupidity of those who ban our historical documents from the classroom?

The teachings of the very documents that insure our independence as a nation and guarantee our rights as Humans and Americans, have been determined unconstitutional. After a lengthy court battle and then the appeals process, the 9th district court will undoubtedly rule in favor of the principal and school board who "Had the courage" to stand up against Christian indoctrination. I guess after removing Christ from Christmas and God from the Pledge of Allegiance, this would be the next logical step, but I must admit that this latest swipe at common sense surprised even me!

Got time for another one? Look at the way the Boy Scouts have been treated over the past couple of years. First, it was decided by the Boy Scouts of America that they didn't want homosexual deviates (does the recent scandal in the Catholic church ring any bells?) in charge of large groups of otherwise unsupervised boys. Then they came under fire because their motto includes the word God. Well, I just can't believe the Boy Scouts have been around year after year and decade after decade with beliefs like these. It's amazing they haven't self-combusted as a direct result of their belief in God and the common sense to keep queers out of positions of power over young boys. Of course the ACLU had to jump in and with the help of some liberal activist judges, the Boy Scouts were refused the use of a public park that their group had used for years.

Because of their reference to God, their rational thought and common sense, the Boy Scouts were denied funding from numerous sources, including the United Way, who previously believed it was a good and wholesome organization. Where is the sense in denying funding to a group that tries to instill values in a morally corrupt society?

If it offends the liberals that I use common sense each and every day of my life, that's too damn bad. That's right! I make decisions based on common sense. Decisions like not testing the sharpness of my pocketknife on my arm. Decisions like putting oil in my truck when it gets low. Decisions like going to work every day to earn a living. Decisions like investing in companies with a proven history of success. These decisions should be expected and perfectly acceptable, but in the world of the weird, these decisions are often seen as offensive and insensitive to others.

It should offend *Americans* that the Liberal elites are trying to restrict the use of common sense in the decision-making processes that affect policy and law in our nation. It should anger us all that they've begun to tell us what and how to think.

As stated before, common sense is a threat to Elites. In order to further weaken the fabric of America, Elites must find a non-threatening way to convince us that common sense is offensive, restrictive and ultimately unneeded in their progressive society. None of us ever want to see this happen, but the fact is, it's happening every day in small increments and in little chunks. The chipping away of America's common sense is underway and has encountered few speed bumps thus far. We're giving away the farm! It's hard to give away the farm all at once. It's much easier to relinquish it acre by acre. Remember, if that farm is taken by force, it can be reacquired by force. But if it's relinquished freely, it's lost forever.

# UTOPIAN GOAL NUMBER 16
## GLOBALIZATION

Do you ever wonder why the United Nations has an increasing influence on the actions taken by the United States when it comes to situations around the world?

It's becoming increasingly apparent that Liberals in positions of power here in America, are more willing to follow the recommendations of the U.N. and world "Community," than to make decisions based on our national interests. America is currently being denounced and ostracized by the U.N and foreign Nations for it's decision to invade Iraq, remove Sadam from power and establish a democratic society in which it's citizens can live freely. Thankfully president George Bush has been more concerned with the welfare of Americans and the health of the "Global community" than any global babysitter has been.

In humanitarian aide we are second to no one in the amount of supplies and cash money we donate to victims of natural disasters and tragedies around the globe. Yet no matter how much we do, the global community and the U.N. criticize that we don't do enough or that we are being stingy with our resources. The American government doesn't have money. The funds that the government receives are the dollars earned by American citizens. So, when other countries (who are donating a fraction of the amount that the United States is) criticize the U.S. for not giving enough, they are actually insulting you and I by calling us cheap. Your tax dollar and my tax dollar are going to assist countless victims of one disaster or another and the Elites complain that it's not enough. At the same time they bash Conservatives for the problems with the social security system, the amount being spent on national defense and the national debt. We're just not giving enough to *their* causes. We give and the U.N. criticizes. Sounds like a great reason to support them!

When it comes to fighting the war in Iraq and the greater war on terror, the Liberal elites in this country have been cringing each and every step of the way. As a nation, we have offended our friends in France. We've ruffled feathers in Russia and blatantly ignored the recommendations of the United Nations. We have further angered the terrorists by taking a swipe at their hornet's nest. We've made religious zealots, who implement plans to kill Americans, even more hateful towards us. For all of these reasons and more, the elites despise Mr. Bush, Republicans and anyone else who puts America's wellbeing above the respect of France and the religious beliefs of enemy nations.

Of course we now know that the reason France and the U.N. were so opposed to us going into Iraq and removing a cruel dictator from power. They were helping the dictator steal billions of dollars from the "Oil for Food" program. The corruption that was eventually uncovered was all the reason France and the U.N. needed to promote the ongoing brutal treatment of Iraq's citizens.

Money was the reason that the U.N. was willing to perpetuate the need for mass graves in Iraq. Protection of their illegal cash cow was reason enough to starve the very people that this U.N.'s "Oil For Food" program was designed to help. It should finally be obvious that the U.N. has no interest in humanitarian issues and that the "Global community" wants only what is good for it's leaders and not it's citizens.

These are the people who Americas elitist leaders want to trust and assist. It's simply a global view of how the left in America want this country to look like in the not-so-distant future. If the elites can rule the world then why the hell shouldn't they be in control of the United States of America? If they could eliminate the stubborn Republicans and flag-waving yahoos who still believe in freedom and individual rights, the world would be closer to perfection. If only these patriotic simpletons would realize that they're the only thing standing between America's peace with terrorists and respect from France.

The U.N. receives great respect and biased reporting from our nation's media. The left loves the U.N. because they protect against atrocities being committed around the world. The U.N. funds economic programs to help starving citizens of oppressed nations. They keep world peace by providing peacekeepers, holding talks and creating treaties. They are a pacifist's dream. Of course they accomplish very little because they are corrupt and afraid of ruffling feathers or offending any one of it's member nations. So round and round the talks and negotiations go, with an actual resolution to a given problem, only a theoretical goal. The end result is of little importance as long as an effort to resolve a problem is pursued. No solution? No problem. We'll just shelf it for now and get back to it when we think we need to.

The American government sees things differently. At least those currently in power do. If a problem or situation arises that does, or has the potential, to harm the interests or security of the United States, we first negotiate. If no resolution is agreed upon and the threat to our nation still exists, we take action. Action, pro-active, and pre-emptive are words that the U.N. despises because they have the possibility of resulting in actual action taken. Action taken means conflict and as we all know, conflict is to be avoided at all costs; regardless of a justifiable need for action to be taken. As competent as the U.N. claims to be at resolving conflict without the use of force, I'm curious as to why the terrorists are still acting so violently. Couldn't Coffe Annan arrange meetings with terrorist leaders and explain to them how ridiculous and unnecessary all this silly violence is? After a couple of days of talks they could begin to understand each other's beliefs and start the peace negotiations, realizing that all societies are different and tolerance is the alternative to violence.

In the new utopia, we can rest assured that the all-knowing and all-caring leaders of the United Nations will insure our national security. We'll be fortunate to have the negotiating power and compromising skills that the U.N. leaders have to offer. We would be wise to turn our military and financial resources over to the U.N. as they are far more competent to oversee our nation's international policies than anyone in Washington D.C.

Like the Liberals who support it, the U.N. is willing to compromise just about anything to avoid conflict. A lack of backbone and empty threats seldom resolve problems in the real world. Of course I only see the downfall with melding our country with the United Nations. I'm sure the elites could list dozens of reasons why it would be in our best interests to surrender to (I mean join), the utopian world community. It would be a fantastic boost to our relations with France and Germany and it would make us far less threatening to rogue nations around the world. Tucking our tail between our legs and asking protection from the U.N. would be our new national defense system. As long as we were behaving and doing what the U.N. told us to do, we'd never again have to worry about out nation's safety.

Why would anyone who was self-sufficient, healthy, capable and strong, suddenly have an urge to relinquish his independence, well-being, ability and strength for the promise of another individual to provide those things for him? To take all you've worked for, fought for, yearned for and just hand it over for no apparent reason is the definition of insanity. Ask a Liberal if they think we should be more involved with the United Nations and they'll tell you how important it is to partner with them and heed their advise. Knowing what we know about Liberals and the U.N., it seems obvious to me that the reason for surrendering our independence to the U.N is because Liberals are afraid of being strong and taking care of themselves. They are afraid of being independent. They'd rather go with the crowd wherever it may be heading than to stand alone for what is right. Is there any other reason for putting all of their power and strength into the hands of another? Why are liberals willing to give away everything the rest of us hold so sacred and dear?

To turn over any of our nations' freedom or power to an international body would mean that every soldier who fought, sacrificed, was injured, or died fighting for the freedoms of Americans, have done so in vain. There is no room for compromise when our nations' very existence depends on our ability and willingness to respond to those who threaten our way of life. But try and explain <u>that</u> to a Liberal!

# UTOPIAN GOAL NUMBER 17
## AMERICAN JOBS

During the last presidential election we heard the Democratic nominee condemn the outsourcing of American jobs. "The president has failed us in our time of economic need by making it financially beneficial for American businesses to outsource much-needed jobs."

The nominee's wife, who is heiress to a particular condiment food's fortune and whose name is the same, said nothing of the dozens of factories located overseas that produce their product for a fraction of the cost they can be produced for in America. As multi-millionaires, they paid disproportionately low taxes as compared to the far less wealthy president and even the average hard working American. All of this while he claimed America's economy was failing and job loss was a major issue.

What the elites refuse to realize is that the reason this nation has had a history of unprecedented prosperity, is we are a nation of free enterprise! Free enterprise has allowed us to exceed the wealth of nations that have been established for two thousand years and more. This irritates the liberals who find it frustrating to live in a nation of such power and wealth when there are so many other nations they feel deserve these things more than we do.

The refusal to recognize that socialism will never promote a healthy economy, and that taxes will never be conducive to prosperity, has left these elites scratching their heads and cursing those taking advantage of the free market.

Things are good in this country. The economy is healthy and compared to the economy of other nations around the world, it's simply outstanding. Remember that what's good for the country is bad for Liberals. In this economy, it'll be hard for any of them to convince the average American that we are in a near depression era stupor. Doom and gloom just can't seem to get a foothold and this is not good for the Elites.

If we consider the money generated by such retail giants as Wal-Mart and Home Depot, we can see the beauty of free enterprise. Started as a small store in Bentonville Arkansas, Wal-Mart was the dream of a hard working and determined man. Sam Walton realized the American dream. The success of Wal-Mart has frustrated the Elites who find it hard to believe a hick from small-town America developed and introduced the world's largest retailer. Expanding at a rate of over two hundred stores per year, the Liberals should be thrilled with the amount of jobs being created by its success in the free market. Instead, they complain of low-wage jobs and are trying to keep stores out of many of its target locations. Wal-Mart, good for consumers, good for the economy….. bad for Elites.

Being the "Watchdogs" for the dignity and rights of society's working class, Liberals have come up with a solution to pay these mistreated workers more. This plan will serve well to punish retailers who "Exploit" their workers by paying them low wages while making profits. In their infinite wisdom liberals have decided to raise the minimum wage. The Liberals are the ones that have fought for minimum raise hikes in numerous states. Here in Oregon, the minimum wage has been gradually increased over the years and now rates the second highest in the nation. At $7.50/hour, employees of Wal-Mart are making about two dollars an hour above the national minimum wage.

Of course when the liberals lobbied, fought for and won a minimum raise hike, there were some Oregonians laid-off or who had work hours cut. The Libby's now want (and are currently working on) a "Living wage" for everyone employed here in Oregon. A living wage in the state of Oregon equates to a little more than $12.00/hr. It doesn't seem to matter to the Liberals that by continuing to raise minimum wage they're hurting the service and retail workers they're trying to help. More than one small businesses in the state had to reduce it's number of employees and/or had to move full-time workers to part-time in order to meet the increasing payroll costs. Some small businesses just gave up and folded shop. How many *formerly* employed individuals did this create? Unemployment and reduced hours seem to be an acceptable sacrifice to Liberals as long as those working part-time are making $7.50/hr. Remember the Liberals when your state minimum wage is raised by an unusually large amount. Ask the Liberals why a Wal-Mart that used to employ two hundred and fifty full-time employees now gets by with one hundred and seventy people and why customer service is becoming so poor. Then listen to them whine when the unemployment numbers jump.

Big box stores, as they're called, really ruffle the feathers of our country's Elites. Big business, making huge profits and providing millions of jobs across the country, is a good thing for the economy and for the families of those millions of employees. That is why the elites hate them. They are successful, profitable and no matter how much you bad-mouth them, you just can't keep shoppers out of them. Perhaps they feel that these stores offer too many choices or that the retail prices of these items are too low. Maybe they just feel that all businesses should be government regulated or better yet, government run. After all, there is no reason for individuals who have worked hard and succeeded in creating a business either large or small, to reap the benefits of their labor. Only Elites should be allowed to enjoy the rewards of success and wealth.

Is it wise for us to follow the lead of these folks who want to drastically raise the minimum wage in spite of the negative effects it has on the low-wage workers they're trying to help? Should we go along with the people who hate capitalism and show it by trying to hinder the progress of businesses operating in the free market?

Do you respect the Elites who climb the capitalist ladder only to pull it up when they've reached the top, so nobody else can succeed?

Going back to the idea of a "Living wage", we can already see the inherent flaws in the plan. For example, if we pay a pimple-faced burger flipper who's fresh out of high school twelve dollars an hour, what are we going to have to pay his supervisor who has worked there for years? Maybe the burger flipper didn't even graduate from high school.

By paying uneducated and unskilled workers a ridiculously high minimum wage we are tempting young folks who see money as the most important thing in their young lives, to drop out of school or go straight into the workforce following graduation, without pursuing college. It may just be the Liberals plans to keep our youth as uneducated as possible; but I think, more likely, they just haven't thought this living wage thing through.

What company could stay in business if they have to pay the mailroom guys twelve bucks an hour? If they're making that kind of wage in the mailroom then wouldn't it make sense that a secretary would need at least twenty-five dollars an hour to get by? Sticking with the hourly scenario, a manager would require at least forty to start and

Dave Sampson

you couldn't touch an executive for less than eighty bucks an hour. This might squeak by in urban areas but in the rest of the country (see 90% of America) it would be ridiculously unrealistic. Add in the countless other position required to operate a business and you would see doors closing in mass numbers across the nation.

How would non-profit agencies get by? There is seldom enough money for many of them to cover the payroll and taxes they're currently paying. Start a new employee who's job is to collate mailers for the non-profit at twelve bucks an hour and pay other staff in increasing increments up to the director or administrator, and you might as well shut the agency down. Who's willing to donate to a non-profit that uses ninety cents of every dollar on administration costs?

Ah, but the Liberals have already thought about this and are willing to give exemptions to all non-profit agencies. Therefore, all the money that should be spent on actual programs can be. Awfully kind of them, don't you think? There's just a little matter of.....Who the hell wants to work for $7.15 at a non-profit when they can make twelve bucks an hour at Burger King? Yea, no staff means no programs and no programs means no help to those who we're told need it the most. Good plan! Well thought out and thankfully, not yet executed!

When the liberals finally succeed in forcing American companies and businesses to pay outrageously high wages, they will also see their precious jobs shipped overseas by the millions. It seems to me that everything that the Liberals do to promote their ideas, have the exact opposite effect when their plans are implemented. Their plans will inevitably fail. That should be obvious to Liberals but as we discussed earlier, they have banned the use of the common sense that would have allowed them to figure this out far earlier in the process.

# UTOPIA GOAL NUMBER 18
## CLOSE THE GAP

Any time I listen to elites talk, the topic of the gap between the rich and the poor inevitably comes up. The catch phrase of "The haves and the have-nots" is so common in liberal circles that they would be wise to come up with an acronym for it in order to save their breath.

The gap between the haves and the have-nots is real. It's getting wider as the result of numerous factors. The rich do get richer. The poor usually stay poor. This is the way it is and I find it difficult to see anything wrong with it. There are reasons and factors for this phenomenon. Let's look at what the liberals want to do to fix a system that they think is flawed.

The first thing liberals want to do is punish the rich in America by forcing them to pay ever-increasing taxes. Ideally it would be the responsibility of the wealthy to pay *all* the taxes in America. Punishment of this kind ought to make those rich folks think twice about earning such large profits.

The second thing Liberals do to try to "Close the gap", is to condemn the achievers and commend the underachievers. In what sane state of mind do we tell those who have worked hard and strived to succeed, they don't deserve what they've earned? In what sane state of mind to reward the unmotivated in society? Why tax those who work in order to support those who chose not to work? Liberals think that success, self-confidence and pride are characteristics of people who are insensitive to the unmotivated slackers in society. For this reason, Libby's think that those who have wealth don't deserve it and those who don't have wealth, do. So as it was in Sherwood Forest, the left is forever scheming on ways to take from the rich and redistribute that money among the "Have-nots" in our society.

Earlier I agreed that the rich usually get richer and the poor usually stay that way. It seems reasonable to me that a person with money has that money because he's smart and levelheaded. He's probably well-educated and willing to work hard to achieve his goals. It would go to reason then, that a wealthy individual would continue to increase his wealth by investing his money in stocks and bonds. By starting and running successful businesses. By doing exactly what he did to earn his wealth in the first place. Conversely, the poor in America usually stay that way throughout their life. While we can't choose our parents, we can control our future. Many a wealthy man was born into a poor family and worked his way up until he had earned fortune and fame. Unfortunately the Liberals have made living in "Poverty" so comfortable that those who rely on the government to support them, rarely feel motivated enough to work to better their situations. Thus, the poor remain the way they are. Another example of the Liberals instituting a plan that undermines it's own purpose.

They keep the poor, poor by providing them with just enough to keep them comfortable and content with their situations. By keeping them reliant on public assistance you keep them more willing to accept a handout than a job. As we know, once you go to work and start making your own money, the government cuts your benefits. Why buy the cow when you can get the milk for free?

I think that the Liberals truly want to close the gap between the rich and the poor in this country. The way they're going about doing it is wrong. Why do they feel they can "Redistribute" the money I earned by working hard, to individuals who don't work at all? What gives them that right? Why should we lower the common denominator by taking wealth away from the wealthy when we should be raising the national income level by getting the unmotivated educated, off public assistance and into the work force? Bring the bottom up instead of lowering the top down! Instead, we punish good behavior by taxing the hell out of the successful in society and reward the slackers by paying their bills and giving them money. Is it just me, or does this seem a little screwy to anyone else?

Lets look at why the "Haves" are successful and why the "Have-nots" are not.

Those who have earned substantial wealth in America have done so through hard work. They educated themselves and many took out thousands of dollars in student loans to do so. They have focus and are not easily distracted or knocked off course. They're willing to make personal sacrifices in order to achieve their goals. They work long hours and seldom complain. They strive for perfection and always see projects through. These characteristics contribute to the mind-set needed to become successful. As for the "Have-nots", they typically have little more than a high school education and are usually unskilled. They have little drive and find it difficult to complete tasks and reach goals. They are easily distracted and are easily persuaded to do the least to get by. They live for the moment without any thought of the future. They are content to simply "Get by." It seems to me like there are some very real and very large differences between the haves and the have-nots. Bigger than just the "Haves" being wealthy and the "Have-not's" being poor. In fact, rich and poor are just the byproduct of a person's determination to aspire.

The old saying goes, "You can lead a horse to water, but you can't make him drink." Applied to the "Have-nots," we can offer numerous incentives for them to better themselves but we cannot force them to take advantage of vocational training or motivate them to apply for student aid in order to get an education. There are programs in place in every major city and in most rural communities that offer classes, training, and financial aid to those willing to apply themselves and work towards a goal. Initiative happens to be one of those character traits required by anybody who aspires to be successful and seldom possessed by the "Have-nots." Even putting these programs in place isn't enough for the Elites. Elites don't require the have-nots to work to survive and therefore couldn't possibly expect someone to obtain training or an education in order to provide for themselves.

Elites tell us that forcing one to decide is insensitive. They tell us to cough up more cash for those who they feel shouldn't be forced to decide between working and going without. Besides, there are plenty of rich folks to help these "Have-nots" who choose to have nothing. The gap will close between the "Haves" and the "Have-nots" only when we as a nation, quit coddling the unmotivated and force them to decide to work hard in order to better their situations. Did I say force? Isn't forcing somebody to do something they don't want to do, cruel and insensitive? According to Liberals it is. If that's the case, then quit forcing the wealthy in this country to pay the ridiculously high taxes that they don't want to pay! Quit forcing me to take money out of my paycheck to pay for the housing costs of a person who chooses not to work! Force is only a bad word when it's used by Conservatives to create change for the better.

# Utopia Goal Number 19
## Protect your Children.....
## by Killing Them?

It's currently one of the biggest and most controversial differences between the two major parties in this country and it's bound to be a topic of debate for the foreseeable future. Abortion is currently legal and practiced everywhere in the country. Abortion clinics, Planned Parenthood and feminists are the backbone in the struggle to keep the practice of killing your kids legal. Elites favor a "Woman's choice" to have an abortion but maybe not for the reason they proclaim. Is it any wonder that with the total lack of responsibility put on today's teens and young adults, abortion is considered a birth control option when our children make a "Sexual mistake?" It's been ruled that young teenage women don't even need parental permission to obtain an abortion and that the doctors performing them aren't required to notify the parents.

The elite's tell us we're "Unrealistic" and "Stupid" to teach abstinence in schools. They insist on passing out condoms and birth control pills and telling us that *our* kids are going to have sex anyway. I guess we ought to just pass out rolling papers and crack pipes instead of teaching our youth that just like sex, drugs can be harmful to youngsters and can have a lasting effect on their futures. We know that criminals are going to commit crime even thought they know crime is wrong and illegal. Should we give them the guns and get-a-way cars they need to commit crimes? After all, they're going to do it anyway. Would that be crossing the line? I don't think it would even be pushing the line considering how dangerous sex has become in today's world. With the Liberal's dangerous outlook on sex education and their adamant protection of a woman's sexual expression they are creating as many victims as our cities drug dealers are. Is a lifelong venereal disease not as dangerous to the public as drugs like pot and alcohol? How about the wonderful world of AIDS? Passed along from one uneducated sexual partner to the next, it eventually kills all it affects. No birth control pill is going to protect my daughter from this indiscriminate killer.

And then there is the actual killing of a human fetus as an alternative to giving birth to a viable and healthy baby. This has become a form of birth control and is a protected personal freedom. Before I get started I'd like to clarify that I believe that abortions to save the mothers life, or to end a pregnancy as the result of rape or incest are justified. My problem lies with young women who become pregnant as the result of careless sex. Our nation's youth deserve to be better educated as to the risks and dangers of sex at a younger age. After all, it makes no sense to shut the barn door after the horse is out.

I also have a problem with middle-aged women, who may be mothers already, that accidentally become pregnant and decide a baby would be inconvenient at this time in their life. There are so many forms of birth control on the market today that there is no excuse for a responsible adult to unexpectedly wind up pregnant.

Let's not forget that we are living in a "Do it if it feels good" world. This means personal responsibility and accountability for ones actions carry as much weight as a wet paper bag. Liberals who have fought for the elimination of common sense and the decline of morality have created this world. To look around, it's easy to see why teen pregnancy as well as drug use and teenage crime are on the rise. As long as your actions bring you immediate gratification, those actions couldn't possibly be wrong. After all, Liberals tell our kids, "It's your right to be happy." Liberals believe that whatever you do to make yourself happy is your God given right. That logic seems more than a little off kilter to me, how about you? Still, this is the message being sent to our youth in the media, through courts, and in our public school systems around the nation.

It makes sense to me that discussion and education among our young people about the seriousness and the effects of sexual relations would do more to prevent many of the problems resulting from teenage sexual activity. Does promoting the problem to help solve it make any sense to you? Why tell our sons that we disapprove of them having sex and then hand them a rubber? Why tell your daughter to say no, and then put her on the pill? You might as well say here you go kid, knock yourself out! With practices like these it's no wonder our children are confused and can no longer distinguish between right and wrong. Moral contradictions are taught to our youth everyday in our public schools and on television shows targeted at young people. Should we expect them to decipher between "Commonly acceptable" behavior and moral behavior? Not if they never learn the difference.

It was the former President of the United States that told the American public oral sex was not actually considered sex, and therefore he did not have an affair. "Slick Willy" set the moral standards for a generation of young people who now believe that anything is sexually acceptable as long as intercourse is not involved. Some of today's more promiscuous teens in junior high and high school attend

"Rainbow Parties" where numerous females wear different colored lipstick and perform oral sex on different young men to give their penises rainbow-colored rings. Good clean fun according to our former commander-in-chief. How about our teenagers engaging in sexual behavior with a "F--- Buddy?" This is not a steady boyfriend or girlfriend. Instead it's a friend, usually of the opposite sex, that a youngster pleasures him or herself with on a casual, noncommittal basis. Another self-gratifying behavior I'm sure Mr. Clinton would be in favor of. Is this the type of sexual behavior you'd like to see our pre-pubescent and teenage youngsters involved with? This behavior was justified and excused by our former president, the current figurehead of the Elites in America. If this is so, how in the world can we trust our youth to these "Enlightened" individuals? We should all stop and think about what the Elites feel is in the best interest of our children before we turn over our parental and influential control and responsibilities to the dimwitted Left. Hell, I'm just glad to see that the Left still holds our nation's leaders to the highest of standards.

Elites tell us that they will go to any lengths to promote the health and protection of our youth. That their villages will join together to raise our nations youth (Hillary! Need I say more?). They will fight to make the world a better place for our children. They stand for family values and claim to be pillars of integrity. How do they prove these claims? By preaching immorality and promoting unacceptable behavior. By aborting the fetuses of thousands of the same children they've vowed to protect. How does this make our youth safe? This health issue not only relates to the aborted fetus, but also to the mental and physical effects that abortion has on the child or woman having the procedure. Does killing the unborn and injuring our children seem like the "Advanced" or "Progressive" way of raising and protecting our youth? Where are the family values that Liberals claim to have a monopoly on when they're killing future generations by promoting sexual promiscuity, abortion and by attempting to legalize drugs that would ultimately lead to more under-aged sex?

As with so many things the Liberals attempt, the way they go about solving problems simply gets in the way of getting that problem solved. If there were a gas leak in a building I could imagine a Liberal coming up with the idea of lighting a match to find the leak. The point is; Liberals contradict their stated goals with the actions they take to accomplish them.

Think about the way you'd want your child taught. Would you prefer a curriculum that promotes understanding, personal responsibility, and accountability or would you rather have the Elites throw their hands in the air and pass out birth control to your sons and daughters? How will you feel when your daughter tells you she's pregnant and has decided to go to a sterile, cold clinic to have the life growing inside her, removed? It may be her personal choice but that doesn't make it the right one. Will Senator Kerry, Mrs. Clinton, Charley Wrangle, or big Bill himself be there to console, treat and counsel your daughter after she has the abortion they fought so hard for her to have? No, because they don't care about your daughter, they only care about, "A woman's right to choose." It's yet another example of how Elites deal with an issue without any regard to the repercussions their infinitely wise decisions will have on Americans.

Let's look at another way our hero's on the Left are working towards the demise of our youth. One of the many problems facing our children today is their health. Childhood diabetes, obesity and high cholesterol are on the rise among the very young of today's youth. At least one of these health issues affect nearly fifty percent of kids in the U.S. today. As parents neglect to pay attention to the eating habits and amounts of exercise our kids are getting, the Liberals are adding fuel to the fire. Nearly all of today's public schools complain about being under-funded. There is hardly enough money to pay the salaries of teachers more less to supply chemicals to science labs and wood scraps to the shop class. This is probably the first time Liberals have *ever* decided to scale back on something to save money. Unfortunately it comes at the cost of our children's health. It's now obvious that their choice to cut or eliminate physical education and sports programs in the nation's schools to "Save money" was the wrong one.

Growing up I can remember a child or maybe two in each of my grade school classes that was "Overweight." This means a child or two might have been a bit chunky or a little pudgy. Today, half of the kids in any given fourth or fifth grade class is classified as overweight, a third of those are considered obese. This is not the sole responsibility of our government but the slicing of P.E. classes and required exercise programs is certainly a huge factor. Once a class that was required each day, physical education classes are now either non-existent or have been cut to a day or two a week. Sports programs that provided athletic training and fantastic exercise opportunities as well as teaching competitiveness and sportsmanship are a shell of what they once were. Again, budget issues have eliminated or reduced the all-important issue of physical fitness.

It doesn't surprise me that Liberals have cut sports. After all, in any game or competition there has to be a winner and a loser. Liberals despise competition and refuse to label a child or group of kids (a.k.a., a team) winners or losers, better or worse, or good or bad at any given sport. Their aspirations to be uber-politically correct, has produced a generation of slovenly, lazy and shamefully out of shape children. Fewer and fewer kids today can perform simple feats of athleticism. If you attended grade school when I did, you grew up with the Presidential Fitness Test. This tested a student on the number of sit-up's, push-up's, chin-up's and other basic feats of fitness he or she could perform in a set time period. Patches were awarded to those who performed the best and encouraged others to better their scores through physical exercise in order to earn a patch the next year. As cruel as comparing students to each other may sounds, it used to inspire goals and the desire to achieve them. As it stands today, Liberals have eliminated the need and therefore the desire to be a fit young person. By doing so they are grooming a whole generation of new medical clients with which to test their beloved Universal Healthcare Plan. Your kids are becoming the Liberal's guinea pigs!

Is having a generation of youngsters who can't do a single chin-up or run a single lap around the track without stopping, you're idea of a healthy child? Apparently Liberals would rather be politically correct by eliminating sports and competitions than promote the health of our young children in public schools. Just another way the Libby's are "Protecting" our kids.

Of course if we trusted much of anything to the wisdom and infinite knowledge of Liberals, we would have become extinct years ago. It is up to responsible parents to control the eating and exercise habits of their children. For those unaware of the lack of physical education your kids are receiving in public schools, let this be a warning. It's vital to the lifelong health of a child to maintain a decent level of physical fitness throughout their childhood. It will also teach habits that will stick with children throughout their lives. Is this something you want to trust to Liberals?

Like everything else the Liberals get their hands on, they've screwed up again. This time the result of their misguided beliefs is the physical and mental wellbeing of our nation's youth. From the legalization of drugs to eliminating physical fitness, from promoting promiscuous sex to supporting abortion, there seems to be a pattern with Liberal thought. It seems to me that Liberals will fight for what they believe in without any regard for what the other ninety percent of Americans hold sacred. As a huge minority, it infuriates me that they have had such success in instituting their harmful agenda.

# UTOPIA GOAL NUMBER 20
## LEGALIZING ILLEGAL ALIENS

One goal of the Left is to give illegal aliens all the benefits and status of legal citizens. This serves many purposes in the ongoing effort of the Elites to destroy America.

As the melting pot of the world, America has always welcomed those from other nations. After all, none of us are anything more than the Nth generation of immigrants from other countries. The difference between the way our ancestors came to this country and the way today's "Undocumented Americans" are doing it, is that our great-great grandparents did it legally. But don't let this little formality get in the way.

The struggle for illegal rights is escalating every day. As more and more Hispanics enter our country illegally to find work and have their children, the elites minimize and trivialize the fact that they are here illegally. Conservatives have been made to look like calloused and uncaring ogres for not being more accommodating to the needs and "Rights" of those here illegally, giving the Liberals another perceived monopoly on compassion.

The problems created by illegal aliens are as complex as they are numerous. In today's world of violence and terror, national security is the biggest concern regarding the infiltration of illegals into our country. As reported on national news, an illegal alien was caught trying to gain access to the United States through the Canadian-Washington border while in possession of explosives that he planned to detonate in the Los Angeles International Airport. As an American I'm thankful that border security was alert and able to detain this individual before he was granted access to our country, in order to do it harm. In another case, a Hispanic individual while in this country illegally, became one of the most horrific serial killers along the Texas-Mexico border. He committed more than thirty murders (that we know about) in towns that were situated near railroad tracks. Some of the victims were young and some old. Some were male and some female. The common link was the brutal way in which they were murdered.

We've discovered that the terrorists aboard the planes during the 9/11 attacks had obtained sixty-three different drivers licenses from different states. They possessed expired passports and should have been deported long before the attacks occurred but due to the fact they had legal drivers licenses, they were allowed to remain in our country. The Liberals living in their bubble wearing their rose colored glasses, refuse to acknowledge the fact that there are people in this world that want nothing more than to harm America. They also want nothing more than to make it as easy as possible for these folks to infiltrate our nation.

For a group that never sees the good in anything or in any circumstance and always dwells on the negative, it strikes me as a bit odd that Liberals tend to deny that illegals are anything but bad. In fact the opposite is true. Liberals can't find one reason for keeping illegals out of the United States. When leopards change their spots, I become a bit suspicious.

Could it be that by allowing illegals access to not only our country, but to its jobs, driving privileges, health care, and ultimately amnesty, that Liberals have a plan? Could the plan be to use these illegals to further shread the fabric of this country that they despise so much? I think so. In fact it's hard to understand any other reason Liberals are fighting so hard for changing the long-standing term "Illegal Aliens" to "Undocumented Americans" and soon, just "Americans."

Their plan is to soften the rhetoric and warm the water until we're all accepting of people who come to this country illegally. Then they hope we'll become more than willing to give them immediate citizenship and all the privileges formerly guaranteed to *legalized* citizens. The wrinkle in their plan is that most Americans are angered by the proposal of granting everything to anybody who can fly, swim, boat, or walk into this country without any documentation or criminal check. It infuriates elites that the security of our nation is still more important to us than the touchy-feely politically correct way in which they want us to treat people who come here in direct violation of the law.

Another big topic in today's America is the issuance of legal and valid drivers licenses to illegal aliens. California, Arizona, Texas and New Mexico are the states most affected by this problem, as the Mexican-American boarder is the easiest to cross. It affects us all to one degree or another. While illegals are issued drivers licenses, they rarely carry automobile insurance. When involved in accidents they often flee the scene for fear of being caught and possibly deported. The cost to insurance companies is astronomical and results in higher insurance for all of the law-abiding citizens who carry it. This is just one way illegals impact America financially. Another is in the job market. Businesses who knowingly hire illegas to exploit cheap labor are a huge reason illegal Hispanics continue to flock to America. In a time when Liberals are screaming about the outsourcing of American jobs, they should be outraged at the quantity of American jobs being taken by illegals who pay no taxes and usually don't even spend their money in local economies. I know that the work being done by these illegals may not be the most desirable, but putting Americans, currently unemployed and on public assistance to work, would certainly reduce the unemployment rate that the Libby's continually bitch about.

Why should a person who has not applied for, or been granted citizenship, be treated just the same as those of us who are legal citizens? Do we not work hard and pay taxes that are already too high? In many cases those tax dollars are put into programs that focus on providing social services to illegal aliens. Illegals who commit crimes in this country are provided public defenders and tried the same as any citizen would be, instead of being deported immediately as should be done according to the law. The more the left fights for undocumented Americans' rights, the more support they gather from that particular group of illegals. And although illegals are not entitled to vote in U.S. elections, there is little to stop them from doing just that.

By allowing different groups from different nations to gain illegal access to our country, Liberals also create separation of ethnicities. Illegals of Asian descent will undoubtedly find comfort in groups of other illegal Asians. The same holds true for Hispanics, Saudis and a hundred other nationalities. These groups never become legal citizens and therefore never really become part of the American way of life. Factions of these groups sometimes form smaller, tighter groups that are often referred to as gangs. Believe it or not, these gangs can be the catalyst for crime and violence. In California, where illegals are welcomed and absorbed into the community, gang violence is out of control. Many areas of Southern California are hot beds for gangs. Citizens and business owners live in fear of these morally challenged individuals. As illegal aliens travel to inland America, we see the violence and crime committed by gangs, follow closely behind. Small towns in Midwestern states and in the Pacific

Northwest who had never given thought to gangs and their resulting crimes, are now well aware of the dangers these groups pose. Gang task forces in Middle America's police departments were unheard of just a few short years ago. Now, with the Elites promoting the "Open boarders" policy, illegal aliens are pouring into our country and bringing with them all of the societal problems that we simply don't need. This is not to say that some Conservatives (Bush included) aren't promoting the escalation of problems by making illegal entry into the country easier by the day.

In fact, boarder patrol agents are hamstringed by rules and regulations that make catching and returning illegals to Mexico, nearly impossible. I can't comprehend why superiors would give orders to intentionally not patrol certain areas that have been identified as crossing sites. Can you? In many cases we know when and where illegals are attempting to cross the boarder and yet we don't *allow* our boarder patrol agents to do their job. It makes me wonder how serious we are about national security, the war on drugs and maintaining our sovereignty. In a post 9-11 world, it seems to me that strictly and determinately monitoring our boarders would be priority; A) number 1. Anybody entering the country illegally should be detained, questioned and deported. In today's completely nonsensical world we instead, turn our backs to the boarders and actively allow the infiltration of just about anybody who wishes to enter our country. Why do we have laws governing immigration at all if the observed policy is to ignore the issue and it's detrimental results?

The dollars illegals earn are largely shipped overseas and across borders. Little money is spent domestically by illegals and therefore they do little to support the local economy. Fewer dollars yet are paid in taxes by illegal aliens as the vast majority work under the table. At the same time they drain social programs by utilizing school dollars, food stamps and receive free medical attention in the nations hospitals. As concerned as the left is about our "Struggling" economy and American jobs, one would think they might frown on the trend of allowing illegals into the country. Instead, by standing up for the illegals from all nations, the Liberals have earned the support of millions of undocumented folks. This is great for the left because it dilutes the influence that conservative traditionalists have in the country. Traditionalists in this country are at risk of becoming outnumbered. Once the vote reflects the beliefs of the left, the Liberals can start implementing their new utopia where everything will be exactly reverse of the sane and rational world in which we once lived.

There are a dozen ways that allowing illegal immigrants into America hurts this country. This is precisely why the Liberals want to fight for the illegals continued "Right" to stay here while enjoying all of the benefits of citizenship. Remember, what's bad for the country is good for Liberals and the problems created by illegal immigrants are very, very bad for this country!

# UTOPIA GOAL NUMBER 21
## SHUT DOWN THE OPPOSITION

It is one of the Liberals biggest roadblocks. It stands in the way of the Liberal agenda. It infuriates the elites and exposes their plan for America. It informs us and gathers our support to oppose the actions of the wacko left. What is it? Conservative talk radio!

Is it any wonder that Liberals are forever whining and bitching about the growing number of well educated, well prepared and well-spoken conservative talk show hosts? These folks are the absolute best things happening in this country today. It's the tenacity of Rush Limbaugh and Sean Hannity, that Elites are not getting away with nearly as much as they used to. On daily radio talk shows, Rush, Sean and others educate us all on the asinine and destructive things that Liberal elites are trying to do in this country. They talk about things that would otherwise be swept under the rug by the major media outlets. They give us a chance to see what would otherwise go on without our knowledge. These new breed of patriots are exposing the far left and bringing their ridiculous ideas to light.

In my opinion, people like Rush and Sean as well as Mike Reagan, Laura Ingram, Lars Larson, Bill O'Reilly, and a handful of others, deserve the respect and admiration of all Americans who believe in traditional values and pride in our nation. Without these individuals fighting for the rights and beliefs of the common man, the elites would find it much easier to implement their value-destroying and country-subverting plans!

There are also some very good books on the market by authors of radio talk shows and by people like Bill Bennett, Ann Coulter, Dick Morris, Star Parker and others, that really shed light on the liberal plans the Elites have for America. Again, I'm thankful for these folks who bring into light what the Liberals want left creeping in the dark. It's infuriating to the far left that people like these even exist, much less be *allowed* to speak out against the brilliant and exclusive elitists in this country. Who the hell do these folks think they are to expose a plan to the public when the public is far to stupid and unrefined to comprehend it? How are the Elites to do what is in our best interest if talk show hosts keep telling us what the elites actually *think* is in our best interest?

Liberals hate these conservative watchdogs almost as much as they hate common sense. In an attempt to silence these folks, the Liberals have gone to extensive ends. Liberal mouthpieces are constantly bitching to anyone who will listen that conservatives have a monopoly on talk radio and how unfair it is to those who want to listen to America-bashing on the radio.

To combat the massive influence conservative talk radio shows have on the citizens of this country, the left launched Air America, a liberal radio talk show headed by the buffoon formerly known as Saturday Night Lives' Stuart Smally. Al Franken and his innovative show that addresses issues nearly as absurd as "The upside of gay marriage," "Why God should be outlawed," "Why Bush should be assassinated," "How to save the environment from Republicans" and "How war in Iraq is negatively affecting Dictators." While listeners of Rush, Sean and the other aforementioned hosts number in the millions each day, old Al found out that Gloom-and-Doom and Anger-and-Spite radio didn't interest too many people in America. Although still on a handful of stations in the country, Air America should be proof to liberal Elites that they are still a very small minority in this country.

This really ticked off the left and, as with everything else, they tried to blame the Conservatives for the fact that nobody listened to their new-fangled Bush-bashing radio station. Now, they not only hated the Right for listening to and believing what conservative talk radio has to say, they were slapped in the face by the fact that except for a few extremists, nobody on the left was too interested in liberal talk radio. With such a poor response to their effort to "Educate" people, the Left will have to find another way to institute their ideas.

As with talk radio, Liberals hate the FOX News Network. For the same reason they despise talk radio, they have nothing but contempt for the hosts of FOX News shows who blow the lid off liberal ideas and Liberal's actions on a daily basis. They report to us the senseless things Liberals are doing to weaken the moral strength of the nation. They inform us of the actions taken to deny us our right to celebrate our religion. They show us clips of wacko lefties protesting and looking like idiots. This cannot be tolerated! At the same time, FOX News covers both sides of an issue and frequently criticizes both the Left and the Right. Of course Liberals deny that Fox is anything but a mouthpiece for the far Right. The Left hates the fact that common folks have the right to report on the actions of the Elites. They're even more ticked off that Middle America has been made aware of the things they are doing to bring the country down. They think that if nobody is aware of their plan, then nobody can get in the way of that plan. Although they have had control of the media for decades, Elites are now making statements about how the media is being monopolized by the far Right.

The Left thinks there is a vast right wing conspiracy, taking place in the media. With one television news station that reports actual facts, and a couple of radio talk show hosts who point out the wacko things the left are attempting to do, liberals go crazy.

Bitching and moaning about how unfair it is that talk radio and FOX News shed negative light on their cause, has not been effective enough to shut these sources of information down. It is the Left's wish that Americans would simply ignore these "Babbling idiots" in the conservative media who try to expose the elitists agenda.

Unfortunately for the Left, Americans are smarter than they'll ever give us credit for. No matter how many pies they throw at Ann Coulter, no matter how they choose to slander Rush Limbaugh, we will continue to listen to their opinions because we want to know what is really happening in our country today.

It's really a catch 22 for those on the Left. Here's their dilemma. Until the liberal Elites are in power, they will be unable to silence the Conservatives in this country. With Conservatives on the radio telling Americans about the wacky ideas and plans of the far left, the Elites cannot gain power. See how frustrating this must be for the Libbys? We're kind of like the kids in Scooby-Doo cartoons that always have the bad guys saying, "We would have gotten away with it if it weren't for those meddling kids!"

Luckily our Elites friends have been unable to silence the opposition. Don't think for a minute they're going to roll over and give up. It's only a matter of time before a liberal activist judge will side with an anti-Conservative radio talk show advocate and will restrict Rush Limbaugh's show from being aired anywhere outside of the Arctic Circle. Or maybe they'll find a way to fine FOX news each time it reports the truth. I learned at a young age to never turn my back on the ocean. It's taken me a bit longer, but now I know never to turn my back on a Liberal. Just when you think your safe, they'll come at you with all they have and all they can make up. Truth has little importance to the Left and they're willing to say just about anything to quiet those who are exposing them.

Elites believe, that like all of the rights guaranteed to us by our founding fathers, freedom of speech is flexible and applies only to them. It applies to the rest of us only when it benefits them. Their basic feeling is the rest of us should just shut the hell up. Besides, they believe you and I are too stupid to have the right to say whatever we want whenever we feel like it. When we exercise our free speech it really frustrates the Left. Anyone who questions the Left is obviously abusing their right to free speech. This should be no surprise to us as Elites treat freedom of religion and the right to keep and bear arms with the same indifference. The Constitution has served to describe, and in our nation, provide the rights of a free human being. For the Constitution to work, we must observe and respect the content of the Constitution and our Bill of Rights in its entirety. Elites, as the name defines, feel they are above having to abide by some or all of the Constitution, if doing so works to their advantage. These liberal Elites feel they should be entitled to more rights than other Americans and that the rights they exercise are more important than the rights of the rest of us. They fail to realize that every American has the same rights and the same freedom. Upsetting to the Left is that my freedom and my rights are no more and no less real or important than theirs are. How could it be that a common man is given the same importance, privileges and rights as those who are in charge of running the country? What were our founding fathers thinking?

Leaders who made valid points, established America's policies and laws. These points were made and tested to persuade individuals that their ideas, opinions and beliefs were true and right. This is the standard and the practice that Conservatives live up to today. Our opposition on the other hand, has tried to institute a new approach to get their ideas, opinions and beliefs across. They do their very best to ram them down our throats and at the same time silence any views that oppose their own. When freedom is the most valued thing our nation has, the Elites approach of bullying America's citizens simply won't work.

# Section 2:
# Where Do We
# Go from Here?

# 1.
## REMEMBER WHAT IT WAS LIKE?

We need to get back to the way things were before the progressive Elites started imposing their distorted beliefs on our great country. They are outraged if we do anything that could possibly be considered influential to a minority's way of life. Yet they have no problem instituting policy that influences the lives of the overwhelming majority of Americans. It reminds me of an old saying my dad used to tell me when I'd get out of sorts. He'd say, "Your right to swing your fist ends where my nose begins." In other words, you can do and say and behave how you want as long as it doesn't affect anybody else' right to do and say and behave how they prefer to. Unfortunately, all of the proverbial arm flailing the Elites are doing is making direct and repeated contact with the noses of 95% of Americans and therein lies the problem. There is a limit to the consideration we will show toward those who are rude and treat us poorly. When we reach that limit we can begin to fix some of the crazy things we've, thus far, tolerated from the Elites. For example:

Wouldn't it be great to be able to speak your mind again without having to be politically correct? I'd love to say what I mean and mean what I say without having to worry about a word or phrase that might offend an "Undocumented

American" from the Southeast region of Mozambique. I'd also like to be able to have a person talk to me in a direct and truthful manner that didn't require me to analyze and interpret a possible alternative meaning to his statement. A meaning that has been masked by politically correct lingo. Straight talk is just another aspect of our society that has been attacked and overhauled by the Liberals here in America. If they can change the way a nation speaks we should not underestimate the things they're willing to do to change the way our nation thinks and behaves. Remember this point the next time you find yourself (almost subconsciously) looking for the words to state a feeling or thought in a way designed not to offend anyone in the country. Pretty scary the way they've trained us so far, isn't it?

Wouldn't it be great to have Christmas again? I mean a true Christmas without all of the political bantering and debates to decide whether or not the nativity scene should be allowed in front of the courthouse? We could decorate an evergreen tree with lights and tinsel and call it a Christmas tree again. Christmas songs could be sung in school Christmas pageants, and wishing someone a Merry Christmas would simply be a kind gesture, not an ultra-offensive insult.

People who celebrate Christmas would be considered humble, moral, sensible folks instead of insensitive, offensive, Christian zealots who are trying to force Christianity on everyone, everyday.

I'd certainly enjoy the lower fuel prices we could currently be enjoying if it weren't for the greenie eco-idealists and activist judges. They continue to prevent us from tapping into our own natural resources and we're allowing it. We could cruise around in the comfort of our luxury cars and SUV's without being told we're supporting terror and wasting fuel. We could tap into the oil supply in Alaska and off America's coastlines. Drilling in Wyoming and Texas could be increased in order to meet American consumers' demand for fuel. We could all feel the pride of being a truly self-sufficient nation that could efficiently produce and refine oil in order to supply the petroleum products needed to take care of its citizens. Wouldn't energy independence be great?

How about being able to enjoy the benefits of a much better economy if only the logging industry could once again cut and process lumber. Contrary to the greenines notion that harvesting timber will ruin the environment, sensible logging and replanting creates safe and healthy forests. Mills that offer high-paying jobs could once again provide the nation with the building materials we are currently getting from Canada. Plywood, particleboard, 2x4 studs and dimensional lumber would be less expensive for American consumers, and the economy would thrive with the infusion of all the American dollars that Canada is now enjoying. Our jobless rate would drop dramatically as a result of millions of new jobs being filled in every aspect of the timber industry. Do you see anything but good coming from lifting the bans put on logging?

How about going to the movies and not being subjected to watching two gay guys kiss, or two lesbians being intimate on screen? I'd enjoy turning on the TV at night and not having to explain to my child why there are so many shows that try to make homosexuality an acceptable and respectable "Lifestyle." I could go the rest of my life without hearing the now common terms "Life partner," "Gay marriage," "The gay gene," "Civil unions" and "Alternative lifestyle." Can you imagine a society where you no longer have to try to figure out the difference between trans-gender, trans-sexual, transvestite and cross-dressers? We could once again consider people who do unnatural and deviant things, dangerous freaks instead of "Homosexuals." Our children could go to school to learn science and math again, instead of being subjected to lessons on tolerance and acceptance. We could squash the gay-pride chants with the simple mantra of "Straight is great," without being called bigots and homophobes. Fathers could once again buy a G.I. Joe for his son and mothers could give their daughters dolls to play with and nobody would call them bigots or politically incorrect. Kind of the way I remember things just twenty-five short years ago.

Could it be in the future that a business, which makes a profit in the free market, might be looked at as a good thing? Maybe we'll realize that profit is good for businesses and individuals as well as being vital to the economy. Supply-side economics will be celebrated instead of demonized. Remember what that was like? Wal-Mart and Home Depot will be commended instead of condemned. Gains in personal wealth will be looked upon as the rewards earned by hard work and determination. The "Gap" between the "Have and the have-nots" will be seen as a direct reflection of an individuals determination to succeed.

Imagine a day when pride and self-respect kept the need for social programs to a minimum. There would be more resources that could be put towards assisting the elderly and handicapped if able-bodied individuals would get off their butts and work. We could help these folks become motivated, by limiting the items they could access with food stamps. We could help them by restricting the time allowed by clients to receive assistance. We could help them by making education or job training a stipulation of receiving assistance. We could require them to be productive tax-paying members of society by putting a halt on the extra comforts afforded them by current social programs. We could help them by holding them accountable. What a great place it would be if our tax burdens were lightened as a result of the dependants becoming independent.

How great world it would be if job openings promoted competition and encouraged education? What if the most qualified individual was consistently awarded the position? Imagine hard work and determination being given more merit than hiring quotas. This would certainly put all applicants on a level playing field wouldn't it? Ideally you'd think the equal rights folks and the ACLU would be begging to implement a policy just like this. In the future maybe we could do away with these hypocritical groups that contradict their stated goals.

Imagine buying an affordable house. This could be a reality if our courts would reverse dozens of rulings that have been filed by environmental groups to "Protect" our forests. By doing away with these senseless rules and regulations, lumber would once again be abundant and affordable. No more importing expensive timber (a resource we already have but can't use) from Canada and Russia. The cost of materials would drop dramatically. Therefore, the cost to build would be greatly reduced, directly lowering the cost to buy a new home. Wouldn't it be beneficial to the entire country to put our timber industry and mill workers back to work? What a boost it would be to the economy. All of this while simple forest management assures timber resources will be available for generations to come. Someday we'll once again realize that timber really is a "Keystone species" to our economy.

Think of the polite and moral society in which we could live if we could teach and discipline our children without the influence of intellectual child psychologists and judges. We could once again take control of our childrens' futures and limit the amount of damaging influences they are saturated with.

No more judges telling us that as parents, we are not allowed to restrict, spank, raise our voices, listen to their conversations, or limit our kid's T.V. time, without being sued by our children. Society would certainly be reminiscent of a better time in American history. How great would it be to have our youth willing to work to reach goals instead of thinking they're entitled to everything they want? Could you imagine teenagers who said please, thank you and found synonyms for their favorite four letter words? Wouldn't it be nice to see kids that were honest and truly knew right from wrong? Just imagine how much better off our children would be without the Elites imposing their child rearing knowledge on us.

Just think, all of these things would be possible if we would stand up to the relatively few elitists in this nation. Those who have imposed the beliefs of a small group of people to change the way Americans talk, think, act and behave. The vast majority of Americans have allowed themselves to tolerate the Liberals and their extreme beliefs. Unfortunately due to our tolerance, their beliefs have been incorporated into our society over the years and their extreme ideas no longer seem shocking to us. We are being retrained in the way we think and act. It's a well veiled, multi pronged attack on the American way of life. All we need to do, to return order and reason to our nation, is shut these elitists down. If you think shutting a particular group down in this "Land of the free" can't be done, just look at what they've done to our timber and fishing industries, our traditional holidays, our outlook on right and wrong, then use a page out of their book.

By blurring common sense, removing standards of education and loosening morals in our society, Liberals have been able to make the absurd reality and common sense disappear. Lets reinstate the ideals that made this country great. Lets make the Liberals disappear!

# 2.
# A Few Ideas

In my first book, "The Liberal Identification Hand Book," I pointed out how Liberals have turned the way we looked at things fifty years ago into the exact opposite today. If they can convince us that what used to be black is now white and what used to be up is now down, then nobody is too sure of anything. This is the ultimate goal of the Left. By deconstructing the morals, personal freedoms, religion, common sense and pride of citizens in this country, the Liberal elites can start their next social experiment with a blank canvas. This cannot be allowed to happen. Already we've given in to the point that we're teetering on the edge of a semi-socialistic society. Any further erosion of our foundation will ensure that the America of tomorrow will be unrecognizable to anyone familiar with the America of yesterday.

It's time that the 90% of Americans who are folding under the pressures and intimidation of the other 10% in this country, stand up! We need to refuse to be bullied by the Elites who feel superior to the rest of us! If we are not adamant about preserving our values and ideals, they will be lost in the liberal sea surrounding the good people of this country.

Personally I think we should be inviting more of these Elites to move to Canada or France where their views are widely accepted. I'd be more than willing to request relocation brochures from these countries for any and all who want to move to these "More enlightened" lands. Lets put our foot down and squash any hope these folks have of converting our great nation to a liberal utopia. Let's tell these traitors that we are sick of them badmouthing every single thing our leaders do to make America a safer place to live. Let's call them unpatriotic when they burn the American flag and protest the military actions that give them the very rights they like to abuse. And lets not apologize to them when they act offended that we called them unpatriotic. Let's remind them of the definition of treason and re-educate them on the punishment that those who committed treason used to receive. Let's remind them that in many places in the world they would be killed for trying to overthrow their government. Maybe if we let them know that *their* beliefs *offend us*, they'll be as compassionate towards us as they've asked us to be toward all minority groups who are offended by our beliefs. Yea, and maybe Osama will walk into the Whitehouse tomorrow and surrender.

It's the goal of the far left to destroy everything that this nation was built on. Until we are a country without morals, pride, religion and strength, their plan to overhaul the country's government and social structure cannot take place. Don't think for a minute that the Liberals are doing the asinine things they're doing, just to do them. They have an organized and comprehensive plan to create a new and "Better" America by first destroying the one in which we now live. As they gain and maintain future power, it will be easy to implement the plans and policies that will become the foundation of the United Utopia States of America.

The most important thing we can do to stop the erosion of America's foundation is to make ourselves aware of what is happening in the political world around us. By being informed and knowledgeable about current events, we can form opinions and take action for or against whatever situation might arise. Likewise, your vote is your voice and the most powerful way to let your elected officials know that you are keeping an eye on what they do, how they vote and how they represent you.

It does no good to complain about the way things are going if you don't go to the polls and vote. Your vote counts and anyone who doesn't think it does, needs to learn a little more about how our system works. We all need to contact our elected officials and tell them how we feel about important issues like gay marriage, God in the pledge, the war on terror and all other issues shaping the future of our country. Call or right your state Representative. Visit the capitol and talk to your state Senator. Become actively involved with politics and the issues that will ultimately affect your life.

We need to support organizations that have a positive impact on our kids. Organizations like the Boy Scouts, Girl Scouts, church youth groups and many others need our support to keep them from being decimated by the Liberal Elites in America. These programs provide moral character to generations of kids who grow up to be community leaders and businessmen. The reasons the Elites are so determined to hinder these programs has nothing to do with their use of the word "God," but are instead threatened by the successful and confident young adults these organizations produce.

I think we all remember what *right* is. Good behavior, moral fortitude, compassion for others, manners, accountability for our actions, pride, strength and work ethic are things you and I still believe in and aspire to live up to. Elites despise these character traits and have been doing everything they can think of to compromise and destroy them. Our youth today have a very watered down concept of what right is, because the Elites have done a good job of blurring the whole concept. If we don't spend more time with our own children and instill the values that *we* were raised with, the generations that will follow ours will be poor quality Xerox copies of moral compromise that will get progressively worse over time.

We have to continue to be unwavering in the way we run our households and the decisions we make concerning our actions and language. We need to show our children that a person can be intelligent, kind and moral and still fit into society. We need to remind our children to live up to higher standards than are being set by leaders in our schools, government, sports and entertainment. We need to tell our kids that athletes, actors and musicians are only role models if they behave like role models. Anymore it seems that if a person can get through the day without cheating, stealing, getting high or killing somebody, society considers them to be well behaved. To me it seems like nothing more than the behavior demanded of inmates in a prison.

We need to tell the Elites who despise this country, that we as Americans will do whatever it takes to protect and preserve our country and our way of life. It's up to you and I to stand up and fight for the best interests of *our* country and to forget about the respect we may lose from the French or the UN by protecting ourselves. No longer can we afford to stand by while Elites take Christ out of Christmas and God out of our society. A country without God is a breeding ground for chaos! It's time to say no to the forced acceptance of gay marriage and to the legalization of mind-altering drugs! We need to re-instill values in our children so they too can grow to be strong moral leaders of the greatest nation on earth! We have to be a nation united and deny Elites the opportunity to divide us with things like special rights, quota preferences and religious conflict! You and I have to support our nations leaders instead of allowing the Left to undermine our government's leadership! We can no longer accept anti-American behavior as "Freedom of expression" while our nation's security and strength suffer! It's high time we demanded accountability from our elected leaders and remind them through our votes, that their job is to represent *us*! In short, it's time for Americans to stand up for America! If we don't, only bad things will come!

We are at war each and every day right here in America. Not a war fought by soldiers, tanks and planes. We're not cutting throats or burning towns. No, it's far worse that that. The war we're fighting isn't for territory or position, not for our physical lives. Instead, it's a war for the very ideals and beliefs that make America the greatest nation on earth. Our enemies in this war are sneaky, deceptive and well camouflaged. Their tactics are tolerance, diversity and acceptance. Their weapons are submission and weakness, apologies and compromise. This is not a war we can lose. Already we've allowed the enemy to win too many battles and as the war progresses they seem to gain strength and momentum. If righteousness, morality and common sense are to be victorious we need to make a stand and defeat the enemy that is undermining our way of life.

# 3.
# MORE THINGS WE CAN DO

You can start making a difference today by going to work, paying your taxes and being happy. Nothing pisses a Liberal off more than a person with pride, success and happiness.

You can also do your part by staying informed on issues and current events. Make a point to listen to talk radio or watch FOX news a few times a week. This will allow you to see what is taking place in our country that the main-stream media refuses to report on, because it may shed a negative light on the Left. Keep your ears and eyes open for news of the ridiculous, scandalous and illegal perpetrated by our Elitist buddies.

Another thing you can do is contact your local school board when you hear of rules that are truly absurd. We've all heard by now, of classes being offered that advance the Left's agenda while refusing to teach the values that built this country. Christmas pageants are being sanitized of any and all mention of Christ. Asinine stories of school students being sent home or even suspended from school for wearing a cross or bringing a toy G.I. Joe to school should prompt you to attend school board meetings and remind these yo-yo's that we won't stand for their lack of common sense. Teachers who dress and talk just like the students they are trying to educate should no longer be tolerated. Discipline in the classroom for disruptive students should not only be allowed but enforced, to create a more beneficial learning environment. School vouchers should be made available to any parent who feels their student is not receiving a quality education from public schools.

You can boycott the movies and television shows that star the entertainers who support liberal Elites or promote the liberal agenda. Write to the studios and networks and express your disapproval of the content in today's entertainment. You can cancel your subscription to newspapers that are biased towards the left and ignore the actions and accomplishments of the right. Refuse to turn on the big three networks during the news hour and let their numbers guy try to figure out why rating are down.

Continue to stimulate the economy by buying SUV's without feeling guilty like the Left wants you to. Use common sense in your everyday decision-making and don't allow chaos in your world. It's not your fault or responsibility for the Left's gloom and doom attitude regarding the environment. If you can afford the gas and want a Hummer then go buy one. If your spouse wants one too, go buy another. When eco-idealist criticize your choice of transportation remind them of all the trails and dirt roads you can't enjoy your Hummer on because those public lands are now "Protected." Tell them it offends *you* when they get in the way of your SUV while riding their bikes and skateboards down the middle of the road.

Strive to be educated, self-reliant and productive. Independent people with pride and dignity are hard for the Elites to control. They have a hard time gathering and "Convincing" individuals who think for themselves and are capable of forming objective opinions. Be sure you encourage friends and family to be self-reliant, therefore the left will have no bartering power over them.

Encourage the Elites to share their true hopes for America. Let them reveal their real agenda and make everyone you know aware of what these elites want to do to our country. There's nothing better than seeing a Liberal in true form on a talk show interview or in the news. Once in a while you'll see a Howard Dean freak out and lose his mind. Didn't all conservative Americans love to see the ridiculous contradictions of the fearless John F. Kerry, during his presidential bid? Allow your friends and neighbors to experience Hillary screaming at the top of her lungs in an attempt to convince everybody that she really is patriotic. When Liberals show their true colors, pay attention!

Form or join groups that petition and gather signatures to put measures on state and local ballots that would reverse some of the senseless laws and policies put on the books by the Elites. "What can be done, can usually be undone." Fight the Elites with the same tactics they've used to deconstruct our society. Work to undo the laws and policies that negatively affect the way we live, just as the Elites have put into place policies that have undermined the fabric of America.

We can encourage legislation that would allow parents to use school vouchers to send their kids to private school where morals and values are promoted instead of discouraged. Where it takes half the amount of money per year to educate a child in a way that that child could never be educated in a public school. After 90% of the school body was enrolled in private schools, the Liberals would have few influential minds left to corrupt.

Hold fast to our history and surrender none of it to those trying to re-write our nation's past. In many subtle and some not-so-subtle ways, Elites are trying to reshape the history of our country so it reflects the future that they so desperately want. We need to stand proud and defend the actions that our predecessors took to defend and strengthen the United States. The sacrifices made by those in our past are reminders of why it's so important to uphold the highest standards for our nation in the future. Be sure to remember, remind and be proud!

Don't be afraid to speak your mind, the Liberals aren't. They've tried to convince us that speaking the truth should be frowned upon due to the truth's potential to offend someone. The only people they are *not* afraid of offending is ninety percent of Americans. Let them be offended, it's their right. At the same time it's my right to call a Christmas parade just that; and not a "Holiday Festival." I'll call a traitor a traitor and not a "Patriot with self-expression issues." You should too. When a Liberal lies let them know you think they're lying and that you refuse to condone their lies as "A series of misunderstandings."

# 4.
# VOTE FOR A LIBERAL?

Until the Elites are in control of the country they must follow the election procedures in order to be voted into public office. For the time being we are still able to decide whom best represents our opinions and beliefs. Likewise, those who side with liberal beliefs vote for the Elites they think will make the world a better place. I tell the Liberals that I know to go ahead and vote for those whose goal it is to institute the liberal agenda. That's right go ahead and vote for a Liberal if:

- You're tired of having military superiority over other nations.
- You agree that the UN should be in charge of our national decision making process.
- Terrorism is acceptable to you.
- You want to see the schools continue to lower educational standards.
- You're tired of patriotism and pride.
- You want to see personal freedoms disappear.
- You think your rights are less important than those of minorities.
- You're more concerned about respect from the French than about our national security.

- Morality and integrity don't concern you.
- Freedom seems overrated.
- You don't mind your kids doing drugs and want my kids to have the right to choose to do drugs if they want to.
- You'd like to pay higher taxes.
- You'd like to see more public lands be off limits to the public.
- You have no use for personally owned firearms.
- You think we're too tough on criminals.
- You don't think any foreigner entering our country should be considered illegal.
- Thoughts of capitalism and prosperity turn your stomach.

Yea, go ahead and vote for a Liberal if you're tired of living in the greatest nation on earth and you desperately want to undermine its success. Your vote is imperative to further deconstruct the most envied and prosperous nation in the world. A vote for the Left will promote the reversal of power in the United States. It will be a show of support for the deconstruction of morality and ethics. It will help to further the confusion of right and wrong among our youth. It will reverse the actions taken by past generations of patriots to keep our nation independent and free. It will ensure that the citizens of America will become dependant on the government for their basic needs. It will tell everyone that you distain Christ and Christianity. It will provide special rights for every conceivable minority group and deny rights to you and I. It will embolden other nations to challenge and threaten us. This is what I tell people when they want to vote for a Liberal. As you may have noticed, I'm not the Lefts' favorite person. But then again, I can't stand them either!

Did our forefathers sacrifice everything they had, including their health wealth and safety of their families, to establish a nation that within a couple hundred years would self-destruct? Every soldier that ever fought for and died for the freedom and beliefs of this country on the battlefields in Europe or Asia will have done so in vein if we turn America over to the Left. Patriots will be forgotten and our sovereignty will be forever lost if we succumb to the Liberals agenda. The stability of governments around the entire world will be weakened and conflicts among the worlds nations will escalate. Chaos will reign and any peace will be brief and inconsistent. This is exactly what the Liberal agenda would result in. Talk about Armageddon!

What else would occur as a result of Elites running the country? We sure wouldn't have to worry about voting anymore. Elites could do away with free elections and just appoint themselves into positions of power. We certainly wouldn't need term limits either. They are restrictive and interfere with dictatorial rule. We would soon be referred to as subjects instead of citizens and personal freedoms would fall like dominoes. Personal wealth would be reserved for government officials and anything deemed necessary, would be provided by the government. Why do people from dictatorships and communist-ruled countries strive and fight for the institution of Democracy in their countries? They've lived in the world that the Elites in this country are striving for. They didn't like it!

Be sure your friends and family know exactly what they they're condoning if they abstain from voting or if, God forbid, they vote for the liberals in their next local, state or national election. Currently and for a reason unknown to me, Mrs. Clinton holds a great appeal for hundreds of thousands of Americans. If support for her grows leading up to the 2008 elections, we could be in a lot of trouble. If the thought of a woman president seems more important to them than what that woman believes in, explain to them the damage that could be done in our country. Forget the warm, fuzzy feeling of equality they're shooting for and tell them to weigh the repercussions of a vote for an Elite of any gender.

We're lucky that a majority of Americans still vote in favor of common sense and for the good of our nation. With a lot of hard work and a little luck we may be able to increase the number of Americans who vote this way. It's important that the Liberals are never allowed to institute their progressive plans for this nation. They've had fifty years to screw things up. Now its time for us to make things right again.

Better yet, lets just send these Elites to a country that abides by their "Progressive" beliefs. There's no reason to try to convert a nation of ethical, moral, religious, proud, powerful, compassionate, good people when France has open borders. Instead of creating a drastically flawed "New America", think of the frustrations, emotions and money these dimwits could save by just flocking to a country that is already doomed to self-destruct.

# 5.

## NEVER BE COMPLACENT

I have friends who feel that conservatives are winning more battles than we're losing right now. To them, this is enough. They have lost concern over issues that could seriously affect the way they live in the near future. They tell me that everything is "Okay." now that President Bush has been re-elected. They have relaxed their guard against the Liberals and their agenda for America. Don't make the same mistake!

With Conservative leaders in the Whitehouse, the House of Representatives and in Congress, it's more important than ever to deny the Left the injunctions, bans and special rights that they push for every day. We must use the power of Conservative leadership to insure future domestic tranquility and superiority for America. Let's give the Left a taste of our agenda. The agenda to promote real education by raising standards in schools. To emphasize morality and ethics. To stand up for individual rights. To nominate judges with our best interests in mind. To continue the traditions that formed and sustained this nation for more than two centuries. This agenda, not that preached by the Left, will insure our future success as a nation.

It's when good men do nothing that bad things happen. By not being vigil and furthering support for American values, those who want to do harm to our nation will get a foothold and create chaos among us. We cannot allow this to happen by resting on our ample rear-ends and being content that we've temporary retained power in the Whitehouse. We must keep pressing for freedom and sensibility, for righteousness and morality.

We can't be satisfied that *most* schools are allowed to have Christmas pageants when an increasing number of schools are crumbling under the pressure of special interest groups to halt Christmas. We can't continue to promote adversity and show tolerance to things when those things get in the way of a healthy future for our children and our country. We must continue to call the Left on the carpet when they try to deceive and manipulate situations in order to implement back-door policy. We've got to stand up for our right of freedom of religion and let there be *no question* that Judeo-Christian beliefs will continue to be the major force in the shaping of this country. We must fight for our right to be free and not just for our freedoms. This means not allowing certain groups special privileges, and other groups different ones. Stop the divisions of race, sex and culture by putting a stop to different rights for these different groups.

Always remember that American citizens don't have freedoms, we are _free_! We've been slowly conditioned to forget what freedom is, due to ever-restrictive laws and guidelines, to the point that we now feel gracious when we're *allowed* to do what we damn well ought to be able to do.

An example; permits to carry a weapon with which to protect ourselves. We all have the right to bear arms, yet due to repeals of our rights witch guarantee our freedom, we feel privileged to pay the government for a permit to carry a weapon in states where it's even allowed.

We cannot continue to relinquish our freedom in exchange for freedoms. If we do, we'll live in accordance with the newly established rules that allow us certain privileges instead of living in a free society ruled by common sense. It's time to say "No more", to laws and regulations that strangle and suffocate the rights of American citizens. It's also time to stand up to the Elites who are doing everything they can to guarantee special rights to minorities.

We must ask, "Are minorities first Americans or are they Asia-Americans, African-Americans, and Middle Eastern-Americans?" In America, our citizens are called Americans, and should all be guaranteed the same rights and be required to follow the same laws as any other American.

We need not stand by and listen to the insults being thrown at our president and our nation's leaders. The Elites are professional name callers and downright liars when it comes to dealing with Conservatives whose opinions and beliefs differ from their own. Yet these are the same folks telling us that we need to be tolerant. What Elites fail to recognize is that George Bush *is* President. They don't seem to understand that he *is* President for the simple reason that a majority of Americans voted for him. So…when they insult Mr. Bush aren't they also insulting all of us idiots who voted for him? They want to win us over by insulting those of us who already don't like them? Wow - and this makes perfect sense to a Liberal.

We don't have to listen to their complaints and name-calling. It's childish and at times, downright unpatriotic. Of course they have the right to say what they want, but they don't have the right to make anybody listen to them. How do we not listen when they are constantly bad-mouthing everything the president does? Turn the channel. Cancel the paper. Boycott their movies and music. Don't buy their books. Do these things to make a point and let them know why you're doing it. I recently canceled a subscription to a particular magazine that I found continually demeaned the president due to their extremely liberal columnists. I wrote a letter letting them know that I was canceling my subscription to their otherwise decent magazine because of far left leaning stories and Bush-bashing America-hating comments. Granted, one subscription cancellation will not a magazine break, but if a hundred thousand people wrote to say why they were canceling, it may start to have an impact on the magazines content. Adapt or die, right?

Also, my wife and I refuse to "Tune into" any of the numerous Hollywood awards shows. We will not contribute to the "Viewer ratings" by watching plastic bubble people being congratulated by other plastic bubble people. Hollywood actors and directors are, for the most part, Liberals who proudly and loudly voice their political opinions when they should be doing nothing more than entertaining America. In return, I very quietly voice my opinion alongside millions of other Americans by not watching their glamour-fest. Each year the rating for these back-slapping, self-congratulating shows declines. Do actors in Hollywood give a damn that I wear Wranglers and work shirts to my job in Southern Oregon while putting in my forty hours a week? Hell no! Why should I care who is wearing whom while working in exotic locations a couple months a year. Do I care which American hating actor or actress recently moved to France or Canada because of our government's foreign policy? Why do we continue to support their success by watching their films? They criticize capitalism and condemn the greed of everyday Americans, while at the same time banking their millions. Then they move to a foreign country where they badmouth America. "Screw 'em" is the attitude I've personally taken when it comes to just about anything Hollywood.

Make a statement. It's easy and actually a little gratifying. Stand up the Elites who feel that "Average" Americans voice simply doesn't count. If we stand by and allow the things we disagree with to continue to happen and if we do nothing to change the things that are undermining our way of life, we will become citizens (or subjects) of a new and much different society. Let's not allow this to happen.

We need to be active and we need to be strong. If you're a good parent, you put your foot down when your child challenges your rules or behaves in an inappropriate manner. As good citizens of America, we must do the same thing when legislators act inappropriately and when judges challenge and change laws to fit their agendas. Never can we be complacent. To do so is to allow the Elites a huge advantage in the battle for America!

# 6.

## SPEND MORE OF *YOUR* MONEY

We should all be patting Mr. Bush on the back for his hard work in the area of tax relief and tax refunds. I know it's totally incomprehensible to the Left that Americans would want to keep the money they earn. They could instead be handing it over to the Elites to run their social programs. Yet it's true. Working Americans feel we're paying unreasonably high taxes as a result of years of liberal rule. The money returned to me by Bush's tax cuts made a difference in my household and in the households of millions of Americans in numerous tax brackets across the country. I hope these tax cuts will be permanent and that the American people will fight the next time the government proposes to raise our taxes again.

Never has a country been taxed into prosperity. In fact, when countries overtax their citizens to pay for greedy dictators and other less motivated citizens, the country fails. Look at any communist country in the world and you'll see that they all end up in shambles, but not until after serious riots, violence, human atrocities, starvation and general mayhem ruin the country. Unfortunately the Elites in America think they will be the exception to the rule. They believe they'll be the one government in history who can tax the workingman to death and by doing so, establish and run a happy and prosperous nation. This is just another reason I think Liberals are totally delusional!

If the Libby's are truly a party of the workingman then they should let the working- man keep the money he makes. If this means cutting the substantial fat surrounding our social programs due to lack of funding then so be it. Better yet, why doesn't the American public ask those who tax us, to volunteer more of their paychecks to keep the social programs rolling along? Why haven't we heard of a single one of these lefties, who benefited from the tax breaks, sending their tax return check back to the government with a note saying "Please apply my refund to the national debt", or "Forward my refund check to a poor minority family in the South?" Hell no, they go out and do what they don't want the rest of us to do with our refunds; they spend the money and stimulate the economy. Why don't we force Liberals to do just that? Send their money back to the government they criticize for not taxing us enough. It seems only fair since they force us evil Conservatives to pay taxes for their beloved social programs.

When it comes time to purchase that new T.V. set or upgrade the family car be sure to give your business to companies who support your community and the local economy. Find out what beliefs the businesses in your neighborhood support. Do they, as a corporation, support eco-idealist groups or the timber industry that supports local employment and industry? Do they send employee contributions to Liberal cause campaigns that further the ruin of America, or to worthwhile groups that promote positive outcomes?

It's important to consider who you want to give your money to. With the money you spend at a given business you could unknowingly be supporting groups or individuals that you would never knowingly support. There's nothing worse than buying a car from a dealership that is owned by a Liberal who donates 10% of every purchase to the, "Elect Hillary" campaign. Talk about a pit in your stomach and not just from sticker shock.

Conservatives know that the more money a family can hold onto, the more they will stimulate the economy by purchasing items and services. Liberals know this too, but will never admit it. They bitch about the slow economy and then vote to raise taxes even higher. Without tax dollars that would otherwise stimulate the economy, we know that the fat in their social programs would have to be cut drastically. This just won't due for a party who wants to be in charge of every aspect of your life, via your dependence on their programs. These programs are expensive and regardless of their actual necessity, you and I are forced to pay for them.

Conservatives believe in small government and personal wealth. We all understand that a certain amount of taxes are necessary to the infrastructure of society and we're all willing pay our fair share. The problem begins when our money is taken from us and then carelessly spent by others. Liberals believe in huge government and therefore no need for personal wealth. They have worked hard to implement their ideals by taking your money from you and using it to create enormous, extensive, bloated social programs that provide everything to everyone. Sounds to me like irresponsible spending of *my* money.

The government can only take so much from the hard working, for so long before the working class decides that its easier *not* to work and join the social programs that they've been supporting with their tax dollars. After time, there will be so many individuals in the preverbal "Welfare cart" that there will be no one left to pull it. Doesn't this seem obvious to most of us common folk? I can't, for the life of me, understand why a bunch of Yale and Harvard educated Elites can't figure this out!

We all need to show our support of the Bush administration's determination to hold taxes down and allow Americans to retain more of their hard earned money. So far we've shown our support by stimulating the economy with the dollars we've had returned to us, and by reelecting G.W. to a second term in office. In the future, we need to support local, state and federal representatives who believe Americans should be in charge of their money and not the government. The Elites are all so willing to spend your money for you, they forget that it really is *your* money. In the future, when you talk to a Liberal about taxes and the need for them, remember to ask that person what they've done with *their* refund checks!

# 7.
## DON'T PANIC

It's the strategy of a party who cannot get recognition any other way, to try to scare you into believing their absurd opinions to garnish your vote. They aren't using force or weapons to scare you, not yet anyway. No, they use the fear of catastrophic system breakdown and play on your personal fears to grab headlines and catch your attention. They've not only employed the technique of lying to push their cause, they've mastered the art of exaggeration.

How many of us have heard increasing reports of "Global Warming?" It's been in the newspapers and on T.V. nearly every day for some time now. The enviro-idealists want us to take note of their dedication to pampering our planet. You and I are aware of the strength and self-healing powers of Mother Earth. We've been educated on the destruction and creation cycles of our planet. Our knowledge of Earth's natural cycle does little to bring attention to the greenies, so their tactic is to scare us into listening to their wacko ideas. We are snapped to attention with headlines by famous greenie actors (Ted Danson ring a bell?) claiming the oceans will be dead within ten years if we don't change our ways. We wait for the forecasted Armageddon with measured pessimism after hearing how global warming is causing everything from earthquakes to indigestion. "Experts" citing "Studies" tell us the ice caps are melting due to human consumption of petroleum products. We're told that seaside towns will be underwater by 2020 if we all don't permanently park our cars. They warn us that volcanoes and earthquakes are more active now than in any time in Earth's history because we've depleted the ozone layer and this is our punishment. Somehow the extinction of every recently deceased species is a direct result of Conservative leadership. Well guess what? We need not panic!

It would seem that the greenies would like us to believe that Republicans themselves are responsible for global warming, a phenomenon that has run in cycles with global cooling for 4.5 billion years on planet Earth. It must be that Republicans have a higher core temperature than our cooler Liberal counterparts, and therefore produce excessive heat that is responsible for the ever-rising temperatures around the world. The only way to return our planet to its ideal temperature, is to eliminate Republicans by conversion to cooler political philosophies or maybe some political cleansing would be better. Greenies also seem to think that we don't realize that earthquakes and volcanoes have been occurrences on Earth since it's fiery inception. In fact, over the course of history these natural disasters were much more frequent and largely more powerful than they are today. After being saturated by biased media, it may surprise you that hurricanes, tsunamis, earthquakes, tornadoes and volcanoes are not natural disasters set into motion by George Bush or the Republican Party. They have, in fact, been occurring naturally for billions of years and will continue to happen when Mr. Bush steps down from the Oval Office. It really infuriates the greenies when we don't panic on que.

The elites want to scare us into global peace by warning us that our "Aggressive" actions around the globe reap only distain and promote violence against the United States. By seeking out and bringing to justice those who attack

America and our interests, we are asking for more violence to be brought down on us. By freeing oppressed people in dictatorships around the globe we continually piss off those who we shouldn't make mad. They scold us and slander our Conservative leaders who have the strength to stand up to those who are used to making people cower. They want us to be so afraid of doing anything outside and often inside our own borders, that we may as well just throw in the towel as a country. Anything we do will bring death and destruction to all Americans. You have to love the Elites self-punishing gloom and doom outlook. They want you to panic and fear for your safety as a result of our international actions.

Why should we be afraid of groups and nations that torture and kill their own citizens? The citizens who can't stand and fight for themselves need someone who can. Enter the United States. Elites don't seem to understand that we really don't care if we anger terrorist leaders as we bring down their networks of murder and corruption. It's not our responsibility to be sensitive to brutal dictators and oppressive rulers. That's the U.N's job. Our job is to stand for what we know is right and just in the world. As a nation of the free, we offer assistance to those who are being brutalized and murdered and to do so with extreme prejudice. Our soldiers join our military voluntarily and believe in the strength and preservation of our nation. The same nation that the Elites despise for not giving in to the U.N. and who apologize for our actions of good around the world. We've been called arrogant because we are the strongest, surest, safest, most powerful and compassionate nation on the face of the earth. That's not arrogance, that's the truth. So when you hear the Liberals telling us that if we keep doing what America does best, we'll piss off the "Enemy" and bring their wrath down on us, don't panic! Its just more elitists trying to undermine what America stands for and believes in.

Another thing the Liberals are constantly trying to scare us with is the economy. To listen to the pessimists (also known as Liberal leaders) on political talk shows and in news articles, you'd think our nation was just a step or two away from food lines and rationing. They remind us of the "Starving" citizens right here in America and that our nation's elderly population are all one prescription pill away from death. Things are so bad financially that another stock market crash could happen any given Monday. Of course, like with the natural disasters, all of this is directly related to Republican leadership. None of it is true, but that is of little consequence. Truth doesn't cause panic like outrageous headlines do.

We can rest assured that our economy, contrary to the media reports, is thriving and growing with new technology every day. Advances in micro-technology, medicine, energy development and a hundred other fields, gives investors thousands of investment options. When they remind us of the starving citizens of our nation, I remind them that nobody willing to go to a food bank or soup kitchen or make a phone call if unable to get out, will go hungry. The elderly have services available to them that were not around in the not so distant past. The new prescription drug plan and medical insurance options make the golden years much more comfortable than they've ever been. And a stock market crash? The fed keeps raising interest rates to offset inflation. We lower rates when times are bad and the economy is struggling. Rates have been on the rise for two years as the result of a strong and growing economy. The best thing you can do to counter their scare tactics is to continue to invest and support the economy by continuing to live your life as you always have. Just look at the things they'll try to do when they find out their scare tactics aren't panicking anyone.

Panic and fear are tools used by the Elites across the country to scare you and I into listening to their half-cocked ideas and plans. They hope by making current events seem like doomsday crisis's that we'll suddenly open our eyes and give their opinions and ideas merit where none is actually deserved. We must remember that when we hear the negative stories about our progress in the war on terror, how global warming is killing the planet, that we are bordering on another depression era, or that by protecting our interests as a nation we're bringing the wrath of terrorists and the hate of the world down on ourselves, it's just a cry from Liberals who feel they're not being paid enough attention. Lies, exaggerations and outrageous headlines are the tactics for the Left. Shock, outrage, fear and panic are the desired outcomes from these stories and your support is the hopeful end result of their tactics. Don't allow them to railroad you like this. Stay informed and educated on current events and world news so you're not susceptible to stories concocted by a political party willing to do anything to regain power.

# 8.
## STAY FOCUSED

With the sheer number of issues on the plate of Americans today, it's easy to become distracted and lose focus on particular things that demand our attention. We're bombarded with news stories about natural disasters, global warming, the war on terror, environmental issues, the nations economy and a dozen other things every night on the news. It seems overwhelming and it can be intimidating to try to address all of the issues at once.

The best way I've found to keep up on the events shaping our nation and our world is by tuning into talk radio during the week while I'm at work. Hosts like Limbaugh, Hannity, O'Reilly, Larson and dozens of others allow a comprehensive look at issues over the course of two or three hours where the nightly news covers an issue in a matter of minutes. Understanding issues that affect our national policies and impact our lives is the responsibility of all Americans. The old saying that starts, "When good men do nothing" is the perfect example why it's so important for us to keep up with the events happening around us every day. To say that the things that take place in your world do not affect you is naïve, at best. At worst, it allows those who wish to undermine America a little more advantage in their scheme to advance their agenda.

We need to keep our nose to the grindstone when it comes to defending the traditional values of this country. We can't afford to lose focus and relinquish the very beliefs that have allowed this country to thrive and succeed. We've seen what happens when we allow the Liberals a foothold in our political and social world. They distort and twist our national fabric until it becomes unrecognizable. By doing so, we lose things that we should fight to keep and we gain things that we should reject and strive to prevent. What kind of "Things" am I talking about here? Lets start with God being challenged in the pledge and removed from school Christmas programs. If we don't fight for our belief in the importance of God in our nation, He will be removed from the public forum forever. That's a loss, what have we gained? Liberals have blessed us with the social acceptance of the gay lifestyle in our schools, on television and our nation in general. It's something we gained that we really didn't want and that harms our society. Lost is the right for Americans in numerous states to carry a firearm for personal protection. Gained are numerous anti-gun laws that we don't want and that weaken the freedom granted to the citizens of this country. Taken from our nation has been a pride in America resulting from our superior economy, government, military and morale. In its place are apologies and compromises that are dangerous to our status as the world leader. Did you want any of this?

Lets stay focused on what Liberals try to accomplish. Just about everything they try to do should alert us that they're up to something that most of Americans won't agree with, and is most likely something we need to stand against. I'm not talking about the actions of "Just left of center" Democrats, but the extreme left Elites who are trying to completely reshape the structure of America. Every time lefties try to block a judge's nomination, take note. When they try to pass more road-less legislation, you can be sure that there's a reason. Don't stand by and watch when the Elites try to take away your right to hunt or fish or take away more public lands. Allowing them to accomplish any small victory just encourages Liberals and inspires them to push and push until they actually start to shape the way we live. Just look at the restrictions that we live by in today's society. Had we squashed their hopes of implementing absurd policy twenty or thirty years ago we would not be dealing with this ridiculousness today. An example of this is the gay adoption policy in Florida. Florida is the only state in the nation that bans gays from adopting children. Good for them! Can you believe we now live in a country that allows ninety-eight percent of its states to permit such an obviously idiotic policy? Florida will be a battleground of course, until the Liberals change the only common sense gay adoption policy left in the nation, or are defeated by a steadfast state government that refuses to give in.

Focus and diligence is more important now than ever in San Francisco where the ever-progressive governmental idiots are attempting to permanently ban handguns in the city. They're not requiring ridiculous registrations or demanding payment of exorbitant taxes, but attempting to completely outlaw the private ownership of handguns by it's citizens. Of course California has one of the strictest gun policies in the nation already and the senselessness of it's laws are the epitome of common sense lost! The crime rate in California's major cities is proof that restricting law abiding citizens from owning or carrying firearms is nothing more than a thinly veiled plan to simply ban firearms in one of the nation's most liberal states. After dancing around the issue, the Elites in The City By The Bay finally just decided to come out and say it; "We want you to be punished if you possess a handgun in our city." If we allow San Francisco to get away with this, it will open a Pandora's box and soon other Liberal California towns will institute similar laws. It won't be long before only criminals have access to firearms. Once the precedence has been set, it gets progressively easier for the Elites to ban weapons in other states until citizens of the entire nation are in eminent danger of losing their second amendment right to keep and bear arms.

Liberals are forever chipping at our rights while at the same time concocting and instituting special rights for minority groups. We can stop them, but we must make our voices heard now. If we don't, our voices will slowly but increasingly be stifled by these Elitist jackasses.

Let's not be distracted by Liberal lingo and smokescreens. What the Left wants is as obvious as it is absurd. Be diligent, be vocal, be informed and stay *focused!*

# 9.

## BE ACCOUNTABLE

Accountability is one of the character traits I admire most in a person. Ones ability to own up to his mistakes or to take credit for his success is admirable and utterly respectable. It baffles me why Liberals do all they can to remove accountability from everybody's actions. For some reason their "Compassion" for Americans forces them to make excuses for each and every one of them who wind up making mistakes or breaking laws.

My brother-in-law has a great quote he uses to let people know that they need to be accountable for their actions. He says, "Own it." If you lied about taking something that you shouldn't have, "Own it." If you screw up a personal relationship due to bad behavior, "Own it." If you break the law and are facing punishment, "Own it." Likewise, accomplishments an individual makes should be owned as well. There is nothing that boosts self-esteem like taking credit for a job well done or a project done well.

Accountability for one's actions, words and behavior keeps a person centered. What we are finding out from watching Liberals remove accountability from personal behavior is that without it, behavior becomes more appalling more frequently. This social experiment has led to some of the most shocking and outrageous headlines in the history of this country. Over the course of recent years Liberals have taken the responsibility off the shoulders of individuals in our society. From students to criminals and from addicts to leaders, accountability has become less fashionable than ever. The watering down of such an important character trait has lead to many negative effects on our society. It's become so commonplace to pass the buck and blame others that as a society, we may never again be as admired and respected as we were a few short years ago.

There are many examples to show that the removal of personal accountability is damaging our society. Look at what bleeding heart sociologists are doing for individuals that commit horrendous crimes. The first thing they tell us is that it's not the criminal's fault. It's not their fault they got high on drugs. It's not their fault they grabbed a butcher knife. It's not their fault they walked into the room of a sleeping child. It's not their fault they cut that child up into pieces. And it's not their fault they buried the remains of that child in a shallow grave in the woods. No, of course it's not their fault. For some reason Liberals refuse to hold individuals accountable for their actions. They also want to make it wrong for *me* to hold individuals accountable for their actions. Who is responsible for this murderer's action? They'll tell us that it's the fault of the Killers parents or will blame society for what he did. Maybe they'll blame the kid who bullied him in the third grade for his murderous behavior. Never do Liberals place blame squarely where it belongs. Not unless a Republican politician screws up. Then Liberals tend to "Understand" responsibility.

How about accountability in our schools? The question could be asked of both the students and the educators. The current state of our schools is a direct result of the complete lack of accountability displayed by students and teachers. Is it just a coincidence that as requirements for our students drop, so do the grade point averages and graduation rates?

Accountability is almost always a self-realized character trait. This means an individual recognizes and atones for his actions, usually to keep a clean conscience. It's a shame that our youth don't realize that by being accountable for their education they will prosper later in life. There are a few students who *do* work hard and persevere but they are now the exception instead of the rule. These students are usually ridiculed and picked on because they actually attend school to learn. It's a sad state of affairs when a student in our school system is ostracized for doing exactly what they're supposed to be doing. I guess the "Justice" comes when irresponsible students leave high school and enter either college or the real world. It's then they realize they are at a distinct disadvantage to the student who was accountable for their education. They can't spell, read, or even fill out simple applications or paperwork correctly. The lack of an individual's educational accountability has a profound affect on society and directly affects the quality of the nation's work force. Thank goodness there are thousands of gas stations looking for attendants. That is a job that *most* of our high school "Graduates" can qualify for.

Teachers in our public schools should be held equally accountable. I have three children who've been through the public school system. Let's just say I wish I could have afforded to put them in private school. The public school system is a complete failure. There are some good teachers but again, they're the exception instead of the rule. Bureaucrats have relieved the nation's teachers of any and all accountability when it comes to the actual outcome of a student's education. They make a million and one excuses for why a senior in high school is functionally illiterate. They blame the books they use for the appalling test scores. It's certainly not their fault that students can't identify North America on a globe unless it's written in big bold letters. Quiz most high school students in our public schools and they can't even answer what periods in time we fought the Civil War or the Vietnam War, more less the reasons for each. Some kids know who the president is but few if any can name leaders in other important positions of power. Apparently the Vice President, Defense Secretary and Secretary of State are not important enough to take note of. It's no wonder our high school graduates are having a difficult time finding work when they get out of school. They are as unrefined as they are uneducated. Teachers should be ashamed that they are passing students that can't spell, add or write. I can't think of any excuse that can justify this. States are constantly raising taxes and fees to "Accommodate" schools needs. In Oregon, more than ten thousand dollars a year is spent per student in public schools. In other developed nations the total is about half that much. This should mean that Oregon students are some of the brightest in the nation, right? Don't bet on it. Our test scores are among some of the worst in the country, ranking 47th. Money is not the answer to solving the education problem. A little thing called accountability is the only thing that can fix the system.

Still, teachers are constantly complaining that they aren't paid enough. I don't know about you, but I feel that anybody who does a half-assed job while "Working" just eight months a year is being paid too much already. Maybe a teacher's salary should be based on results instead of a teachers' union contract. I do believe that would be a motivating factor for the people responsible for a severely handicapped educational system. Make base pay minimal and offer incentives for percentages of students who achieve high marks. Add ten thousand to your salary if at least eighty-five percent of your students test a "B" level, fifteen thousand if the same percent test at an "A" level. I can guarantee we'd see some accountability from these complacent teachers who are currently just going through the motions.

The American public would welcome accountability. In fact, it should be a little more wide spread among politicians and business executives. I think the act of being accountable should be a stipulation of public service. Businesses would be wise to develop a screening process for detecting accountability in order to hire only respectable individuals. If we would hold people to higher standards, we might just see things change back to a society of responsible and respectable citizens. Can you even imagine what that would be like?

A society comprised of largely accountable people would be a society with less crime and fewer atrocities. Our current, "Do it if it feels good" attitude focuses on the actions and not the effects, of one's behavior. Liberals have convinced us that we should be allowed to do just about anything we want to and it's our right to behave in any manner we choose. That's all fine and good, but they fail to realize that without repercussions for poor behavior or outrageous actions, peoples' behavior will get progressively worse. This is what we are seeing in today's newspaper headlines and television news stories. Our society is reaping the seeds of a generation that has been raised to think of themselves and their immediate gratification before all else. The "Consequences don't matter" generation is the generation that brought you the proliferation of school shootings, teen murderers, the rise in violent crime and increased teenage pregnancy. With at least one generation completely detached from the concepts of accountability and responsibility, the future behavior of our nation's youth can only get worse. It's a grim picture. One that has been allowed to take shape by our Liberal friends who feel personal accountability is somehow cruel or insensitive. I guess now would be a good time to let Liberals know that their strategy for raising our children *isn't working*! Parents must take control of their kids and instill the values and morals that most of us "Old folks" were raised with. It's the job of all parents to provide boundaries for their kids. Parents also need to relearn a word that should be used freely with teenagers. That word is "*No!*" Today's kids are allowed (and therefore expect) to do things or act in ways that would simply not be tolerated in the past. This is great for a kid who seems to get everything he wants, but parents aren't doing their kids any favors by allowing them free reign.

Parents need to be just that, parents. Too many adults with children try to be friends with their kids. Friends are friends because they usually agree with you and seldom tell you, "No." See where this might disqualify a responsible parent from being best friends with their kids? Unfortunately, we have too many middle-aged adolescents with children. They want to be accepted and viewed as cool by their kids and their kid's friends. They don't realize that their job is to be a role model, not to act like their kids. Their job is to teach respect and morality, not to act like their kids. Their job is to set limits and provide boundaries, not to act like their kids. If I did my job as poorly as these liberal parents are doing theirs, I'd be looking for another job. It really is a shame that you can't fire parents. It's also a shame that there isn't a common sense test that prospective parents have to take before having a child.

I'm afraid that after allowing our children all of the freedom we have, that it might just be too late to rein them back in. To go from raising a teenager by teaching him he can "Do anything you want at anytime you want," to imposing limitations and setting rules, doesn't seem likely. Children need to be raised with consistency from the time their young. I can only hope that parents starting families today will realize that the way they raise their children will have a direct affect on how society behaves in the years to come. We truly reap what we sow when it comes to social behavior.

Accountability. It's a word that has been largely removed from our vocabulary by liberal Elites. For whatever reason, the Left wants nobody held accountable for their actions. Liberals are forever justifying poor behavior and making excuses for vile actions. We've seen how our society has "Progressed" as a result. It has never been more important to stress to our children the need for accountability. Without it we'll continue to decay as a society.

# 10.
## BUCK THE BUREAUCRACY

Big government is the end result of any liberal plan. Their end plan; raise taxes to hire more government employees to run more social programs that provide services to more low-income people being overtaxed by Liberals. It's a vicious circle that reminds me of a dog chasing his tail. Much like the stupid mutt, Liberals can't realize that what they're doing is just running in circles. And like the mutt who finally catches his tail, Liberals would certainly yipe if they ever felt the pain caused by the expansion of their precious social programs.

Conservatives already know the answer to the problems that Liberals are trying to solve. It's a bit like having a child struggling to solve his math homework while you look on, already having the answer in your head. You watch the kid think and see him bend his brain to understand a simple equation while wishing you could somehow force understanding on him. As any parent can tell you, children must make their own mistakes. Unfortunately we cannot allow Liberals to make mistakes. The mistakes they would make would definitely run the United States into the ground. Therefore, we must fight to keep Liberals out of power and thus prevent their mistakes from ever being made.

Big government simply doesn't work. Power corrupts and absolute power corrupts absolutely. By giving more and more power to the government, we're guaranteeing increasing acts of corruption, atrocities and immoral conduct. When Liberals demand higher taxes (because we just don't pay enough in taxes now) what they're really demanding is more power and control over you. When Liberals expand social programs and constantly relax qualifications for individuals to receive government assistance, they're really recruiting Americans to become dependent on them. The more they provide for you, the more dependent you become on them. They want a hundred percent control so they're striving for a hundred percent dependence. Why do you think Liberals hate those who are successful and self-reliant in our society? Unless they can break them by taxing them to death, those individuals will never be reliant on the government.

Currently there are too many self-reliant citizens for the Liberals to see their plan through. By continuing to punish the successful through outrageous taxes, Liberals continue to work towards their goal. Until that time, they have to be content with the social programs that are already in place. These programs happen to be so bloated and over funded that liberals should be thrilled at the waste already taking place. They have to actively recruit people to fill the roles available. By consistently increasing funding for programs like food stamps and housing assistance, Liberals have created more cure than there is disease.

The bureaucracy is now bigger than the cause that created it. More dollars are being spent on running the programs than are actually being spent on the programs themselves. Imagine being a short order cook who typically serves ten customers an hour. Now increase those coming in for breakfast to sixty per hour. The boss better hire another five cooks, right? When the customer count returns to normal only one cook will be needed again. Works in the private sector, but not in the land of big government.

In government, funding was requested and granted to supply the kitchen with the cooks it needed to meet demand. When demand decreases and fewer cooks are needed, the kitchen is in jeopardy of losing free money to pay for those five additional cooks. Their solution is to go find people to drag into the diner in order to justify keeping six cooks on staff. Their job security depends on recruiting clients. While recruiting clients in the free market equates to profit, recruiting clients for social programs to ensure funding and job security, is atrocious. It's as shameful as it is widely practiced. Taxpayers should pay more attention to the amount of fat in the government's social programs. They might just realize that they are paying taxes to have five cooks stand around and watch one guy fry an egg. Shouldn't we be a little more upset when bureaucrats in Washington tell us we have to pay more taxes in order to support *another* social program?

Why do social programs require such a huge amount of administration? There seems to be more people working *for* the program that there are who benefit *from* it. It's now to the point that in many cases, upwards of eighty to ninety percent of program funding is spent on administration. I work for a non-profit that spends more than ninety-five percent of it's funding directly *on* the program and only three percent on administration. "How is this possible," the Liberals would ask. Here it goes, Liberals pay attention and take note. I do three different jobs thus eliminating the need for two additional employees. I have the time and ability to do all three without putting undue stress on myself. If I were employed full time and had to do only one of these three jobs each day, my employer would be paying me to twiddle my thumbs four hours a day. My employer would also have to hire two additional people to share the workload of the three jobs I am doing. They too, would only have enough work to keep them busy for a few hours each day. Also, I'm self-motivated because I know I am not irreplaceable and thus strive to be a productive employee. The fact that I don't need supervision in any of the three aspects of my daily work eliminates the need for my employer to hire three supervisors to watch me work. I do my own paperwork, too. I just saved my employer the cost of hiring a secretary for me. So, by filling my day with productive work, by not needing supervision to complete my tasks and by doing my own paperwork I save the company from having to pay for another six employees each month. If I can accomplish this in a small non-profit organization in rural Oregon, why can't our Harvard-educated Liberals figure out how to streamline the government's bureaucracy?

Privately funded, non-profit agencies are required to maximize their productivity to payroll ratio in order to accomplish their tasks. Government programs maximize their payroll while reducing the amount of tasks they accomplish. The reason for this; private dollars are hard to come by and highly coveted. When donations come in, being a good steward of donated money insures ongoing donations from individuals and organizations that support that particular cause. This is called being fiscally responsible.

On the other hand, government funding is perceived by most to be money given to agencies by the government. "Government" doesn't actually have money to give. That's why it needs to create revenue. Not until it collects taxes from working Americans can it distribute funding to social programs. When you hear of budget increases to this program or that agency, know it's a direct result of the government raising your taxes or charging you higher fees. Since we all pay for these programs I feel we should be able to demand some accountability from those in charge of them. Show me some positive outcomes or a reduced caseload resulting from a successful program. If these programs do what they were developed to do, we should all start to see a reduction in our taxes because fewer people should be depending on the social programs from year to year.

Government has a very difficult time reigning in spending once it's accustomed to a certain budget. What they could once accomplish with a hundred dollars now costs them a hundred and twenty to do. To ask them to find a way to get the job done for ninety is nearly incomprehensible. Why? Because they've been "Living above their means" when it comes to running programs efficiently. Maybe costs are on the rise due to upgrading the department's vehicles every couple of years instead of simply maintaining them. Maybe it's having more staff than the "Cause" requires. Perhaps it's the huge benefit packages that bureaucrats fight so tenaciously to get. Whatever the reason, streamlining the system is unheard of. Frivolous government spending is almost as common as a Liberal caught bashing Bush. In fact, we're usually told that if the budget doesn't increase for the next fiscal year, there will be severe cuts to those clients who rely on the program. While these poor folks suffer because you don't want to pay a paltry fifty additional dollars in taxes each year, those in charge of these money-grubbing agencies continue to enjoy their new "Company" cars and annual bonuses.

This is how our current government works. Can you imagine what the "Government monster" that Liberals want to institute would look like? All I can say is that if the Left ever regains enough power to change the way that taxes are assessed and social programs are funded, we can all conveniently hand our paychecks directly to the government while waiting in line for government assistance programs. How "Revolving door" would that be? Kind of like that dog chasing it's tail, eh? Big government equals big problems for this nation. When the government has removed the ability for us to rely on ourselves, we'll be left with no other option than to rely on the government. Our complete dependence on government gives government complete control over us. Remember this when Hillary talks about the need for bigger social programs or Ted Kennedy demands that we pay higher taxes. Don't become a subject of the new utopia! Big government. Good for Liberals, bad for America!

There's no time like the present to send a message to the Liberals in Washington. We're off to a good start by re-electing Conservative leadership, but we must be diligent in our fight against huge bureaucracies and big government that are gaining in size daily. Without huge social programs, Liberals can't get a foothold on their control over Americans. With nobody to control, Liberals can't be happy. Ergo, if liberals can't have control of your life and can't be "happy," they will have to find other goals to pursue or move to a more progressive country. We should all be so lucky! It's not only Liberals who get caught up in the policies and budgets that advance the progression of big government. When your Representatives and Senators are facing a vote to increase or reduce state or federal spending, voice your opinion. When their vote is required for any one of a dozen of social programs, call or write them and remind them we don't want big government. Get your family and friends to call too. If legislators know we're aware of the issues they're deciding on, they're more likely to listen to our opinions and beliefs. Remember that they work for us and with enough noise from individuals, our voice will be heard. If it's too much work for you to keep up on issues and contact your legislators, get used to the idea of living in the United Utopian States of America.

# Conclusion

It's up to you and me to decide what the America of fifteen years from now will look like. We have the opportunity and the ability to shape the future of our country. It's not an easy task, but we must never forget that our forefathers had a much more difficult task some two hundred and thirty years ago. Our sacrifices are our time, our attention and our actions. The sacrifices made by the founding fathers were treason, persecution and death. Let us not allow their sacrifices of pursuing and perfecting freedom and prosperity, be in vain.

Will we choose to act? Will we preserve our nations beliefs and morality, our strength and our sovereignty? Or will we decide that our attention and actions are too much of an inconvenience for our busy lives? Will we allow Elites, with big plans for the future of America, to proceed unhindered with the deconstruction of our country?

We all need to imagine what the America of tomorrow will look like if we don't preserve the America of yesterday. Does the thought of society becoming much more appalling and progressive than it is today upset you? If the further decay of morality and personal responsibility disgusts you, then it's time to make a stand. Let's not idly stand by and watch our freedom be compromised, our strength stripped, our dignity stolen and our sovereignty given away! In other words, lets keep the country out of the hands of the liberal

Elites! Just remember that for every one of these radical anti-American progressives, there are nine of us to deny him his goal of desecrating the nation in which we live.

Go back and read section one of this book and ask yourself if the country depicted in the first twenty-one chapters is one in which you'd like to live. Is it a country in which you'd like to see you children and grandchildren raised? The Liberals who are out to deconstruct this country have already set the moral decay and social rot into motion. It's already started and will continue to fester and spread if we don't put a stop to it now.

The plans that Elites are attempting to institute into practice and law are obvious. Unless we step back once in a while, it's sometimes easy to miss the forest for the trees. We can't afford to overlook any of the schemes and ploys being devised by the Left. Acceptance of political correctness has blurred our vision of their already distorted plans to the point we can't always recognize what we're looking at. It's now time to take a step back and reflect on where we've been led so far. That should be enough to snap us back to reality and out of the land of the weird in which we've been convinced to live. Let's put the breaks on this runaway freight train of national destruction and moral decay!

It's time for all of us to wake up. This book should serve well as our alarm clock. Let's shed the indifference and nonchalant attitude we've shown thus far to the Elites when they demand tolerance, diversity, acceptance, and politically correct speech. We must stand up, truthfully voice our opinions, and be proud of the America that is the strongest country the world! A proud dignified country with citizens who are strong and confident. (Even while writing the previous line I felt that just maybe those ideas would offend somebody. How sensitive we've become to those who are trying to subvert us.) Let's put an end to the absurd and dangerous ideas and policies being implemented by the Left.

These Liberals jackasses are making decisions that will affect the future of our nation! The Ted Kennedy's, Barbara Boxer's, John Kerry's and Hillary Clinton's of the political world are why the Left can't decide on any issue and usually discuss whether the issue needs further discussion. These non-committal and wavering debaters of the obvious scare the hell out me and should frighten you, too. They want us to bow to their intellect while following blindly as they reduce the greatest nation in history, to rubble. Will we allow them to convince us that their plan is good for America?

Make no mistake about it. Liberals simply get in the way of Americas well-being. They have become a group of self-loathing obstructionalists bent on standing in the way of national security and common sense. Liberals attach themselves to such causes as blocking conservative judges that interpret law, instead of instituting a liberal agenda. They filibuster presidential nominees who have a proven track record of getting the job done and criticize those who have served to protect American interests. They abhor traditional beliefs and ceremonies.

Who willingly fights against laws that would protect our boarders? Who actively fights for the abolishment of the word "God" in our society? Who passes agendas that continue to dumb down our children? Who badmouths the leaders who fight for our freedom? Who punishes businesses for earning profits? Who prohibits the use of our nation's natural resources? Who apologizes on behalf of America for being successful and powerful? Who would like to see nothing more than America transformed into a socialist utopia? The answer is one word and it's the same for all of these questions. You know it as well as I do; it's, *"Liberals!"*

Americans would be well served if Liberals would gather their numbers and settle on a remote island where they could implement their socialist beliefs and immoral behaviors and live happily ever after. Instead, they spend their time and efforts struggling to convert our country into the utopia they envision. That country would not be America. It's strange that these Liberals hide behind the very rights that grant them the ability to ruin their own country. Talk about cutting off your nose to spite your face. Are these folks so shortsighted that they cannot foresee the results of their actions if ever they were implemented? I could care less if these idiots destroy themselves but it's our job to keep these idiots from hurting our country. We better stand up as the majority we are and tell these extremists that their actions and behavior will no longer be tolerated.

Only when Liberal's ever-progressive agenda is stopped, and common sense is restored, will the beliefs in patriotism, pride and righteousness have completely positive connotations again. And after all, isn't it our right to be proud that we live in the most powerful, compassionate and morally superior nation in the world? It is for now. Let's keep it that way!

# ABOUT THE AUTHOR

The author lives in southern Oregon with his wife Niki and the youngest of their three children.

Dave grew up in small southern Oregon towns before attending high school and college in California. Upon returning to Oregon in 1992, he took an interest in the shape the country was taking under the new and disconcerting "leadership" of the Clinton administration. He has since been critical of the Democratic Party and their leftist amigos, the liberal elites. His concern for the future of his kids in a country gone to the left, and his desire to expose the rediculous and dangerous plans the left has in store for our nation, inspired him to write common sense political books aimed at all sensible, hard-working Americans.

He's the author of "The Liberal Identification Hand Book," published in 2005.

Printed in the United States
59788LVS00001B/124-135